# Writings of Famous Persian Writers

# WRITINGS of FAMOUS PERSIAN WRITERS

J.K. Tomar

**Mahaveer & Sons**
(Publishers & Distributors)
New Delhi- 110002

First Edition : 2009

ISBN : 978-81-8377-236-5

*Published by :*

**MAHAVEER & SONS**

(Publishers & Distributors)

H-2 /16 Ansari Road, Darya Ganj,

New Delhi- 110002

*Editorial office:*

3072/28 1st floor Gola Market

Darya Ganj, New Delhi- 110002

E-mail : mahaveersonspub@rediffmail.com

**Ph. 23242069, Mob. 9899608339**

**PRINTED IN INDIA**

---

Published by Smt. Seema Sharma for Mahaveer & Sons, H-2/16, Ansari Road Darya Ganj, New Delhi-110002. & Printed at Himansu Printing press Delhi.

# PREFACE

The knowledge which mediaeval Europe had of India and Persia was mostly indirect, and, as might be expected, deficient both in correctness and extent, resting, as it did, on the statements of classical and patristic writers, on hearsay and on oral communication. In the accounts of the classic writers, especially in those of Pliny, Strabo, Ptolemy, truth and fiction were already strangely blended. Still more was this the case with such compilers and encyclopaedists as Solinus, Cassiodorus and Isidorus of Sevilla, on whom the mediaeval scholar depended largely for information. All these writers, in so far as they speak of India, deal almost entirely with its physical description, its cities and rivers, its wealth of precious stones and metals, its spices and silks, and in particular its marvels and wonders.

Nor do the classic authors give us any more information about the literature of Persia, though the Iranian religion received some attention. Aristotle and Theopompus were more or less familiar with Zoroastrian tenets, and allusions to the prophet of ancient Iran are not infrequent in classic writers. But their information concerning him is very scanty and inaccurate. To them Zoroaster is simply the great Magian, more renowned for his magic art than for his religious system.

— *Author*

# Preface

[illegible]

[illegible]

Author

# Contents

# 1

# The Bustan

*Sadi was named by a brother poet the "nightingale of the groves of Shiraz." He was also noted in his lifetime as a religious teacher, though he never claimed to be inspired by any higher wisdom than the human intellect. The first work of this remarkable man was the "Bustan," which means the fruit-garden, or orchard. The book contains the fruits of the author's long experience, his judgments upon life, illustrated by a vast store of anecdotes.*

## INTRODUCTION

*In the name of the Lord life-creating!*

*The Wise One speech-creating within the tongue!*

*The Lord, the giver, hand-seizing!*

*Merciful, sin-forgiving, excuse-accepting!*

A King such that whosoever turned away his head from His door

*Found not any respect at the doors to which he went,*

*The heads of kings, neck-exalting,*

*Are at His court, on the ground of supplication.*

*He does not instantly seize the froward;*

*He does not drive away with violence those excuse-bringing.*

*And though He becomes angry at bad conduct,*

When thou didst return He canceled the past circumstance in the book of sins.

The two worlds (this and the next) are like a drop in the sea of His knowledge;

He sees a crime, but in mercy covers it with a screen.

If a person seeks a quarrel with his father,

Doubtless the father becomes very angry.

And if a relation be not satisfied with a relation on account of bad conduct,

He drives him from before him, like strangers.

And if the clever slave is not of use,

The master holds him not dear,

And if thou art kind to friends,

The friend will fly from thee to the distance of a league.

And if a soldier abandons service,

The king army-leading becomes quit of him.

But the Lord of high and low

Shuts not the door of food on any one, on account of his sin.

The embroidered leather surface of the earth is His common table;

At this open table, whether enemy or friend—-what matter?

And if He had hastened against one tyranny-practicing

Who would have obtained safety from the hand of His violence?

His nature is free from suspicion of opposition and similitude;

His kingdom independent of the devotion of jinn and mankind.

The servant of His order every thing and person:

The son of Adam, and fowl, and ant, and fly.

He spreads so wide a tray of liberality,

That the Simurgh in the mountains of Kaf enjoys a portion.

Grace and liberality diffusing, and work executing;

Because He is the Possessor of Creation and Knower of secrets.

Grandeur and egotism are proper for Him,

Whose kingdom is ancient and nature independent.

He places the crown of fortune on the head of one;

He brings another from a throne to the dust.

This one has the cap of Good-Fortune on his head;

That one the blanket of Misfortune on his body.

He makes a fire, a rose-garden for Ibrahim;

He takes a crowd, from the waters of the Nile to the fire of Hell.

If that making the fire a rose-garden—it is the written order of His beneficence;

And if this—the destruction of Pharaoh in the Nile—it is the sign-manual of His order.

Behind the screen He sees bad acts:

By His own favor He covers them with a veil.

If with threatening He draws forth the sharp sword of Command,

The Cherubim will remain deaf and dumb.

And if from the tray of Liberality He gives victuals to be carried home,

'Azazil [i.e., Satan] will say, "I may carry away a good portion."

At the Court of His grace and greatness

The Great Ones have put greatness out of their heads.

In mercy, near to those who are distressed:

A hearer of the prayer of those supplication-making.

Concerning circumstances not yet come to pass, His knowledge penetrating;

As to secrets unspoken, His grace informed.

By power, the Guardian of high (sky) and low (earth),

The Lord of the Court of the day of reckoning (Judgment day).

The back of a person is not free from obedience to Him (it must bend);

On His word there is not room for the finger of a person (in slander).

The ancient doer of good, good-approving;

With the reed of Destiny, in the womb, picture-painting.

from the east to the west, the moon and sun

He put into motion; and spread the firmament on the water.

The earth, from distress of earthquake, became stupefied;

On its skirt He drove down a mountain as a nail.

He gives to the seed of man a form like a *pari;*

Who has made a painting on the water?

He places the ruby and the turquoise in the back-bone of the rock;

The red rose, on the branch of green color.

From the cloud He casts a drop toward the ocean;

From the back-bone of the father He brings the seed into the womb.

From that drop He makes an incomparable pearl;

And from this He makes a form of man like the lofty cypress.

The knowledge of a single atom is not hidden from Him,

To whom the evident and the hidden are one.

He prepares the daily food of the snake and the ant;

Although they are without hands and feet, and strength.

By His order He portrayed existence from non-existence;

Who, except He, knows how to make the existing from the non-existing?

Another time He takes away creation to the concealment of non-existence,

And thence conveys it to the plain of the place of assembling the Resurrection.

The people of the world are agreed to His divine origin;

Overpowered in respect to the substance of His essence.

The people discovered not what was beyond His majesty;

The vision discovered not the extent of His power.

The bird of Fancy flies not to the summit of His nature;

The power of the intellect arrives not at the skirt of His description.

In this whirlpool a thousand ships of reason foundered,

In such a way that not a plank was found on the marge.

Many nights I sat lost in this journey of thought of God,

When suddenly terror seized my sleeve, saying, "Get up!"

The knowledge of the King is the encircler of the wide plain of creation;

Thy conjecture becomes not the encircler of Him.

Genius reaches not to the substance of His nature;

Thought reaches not to the profundity of His qualities.

One can attain to the Arab poet, Suhban, in eloquence;

But one can not reach to the substance of God without equal.

Because the immature ones have on this road urged the steed of thought,

At the words "la ahsa," they have wearied of the pace.

One can not gallop a steed in every place,

Places there are where it is proper to cast the shield.

And if a traveler becomes acquainted with the secret of God

They will shut on him the door of returning to the world.

In this banquet of the mystery of God they give a cup of the wine of the love of God to that one,

To whom they give a draught of senselessness that he may not utter the mystery of God.

The wise man fears this sea of blood the mystery of God,

Out of which no one has taken the bark of his life.

Of this hawk, the eye is sewn up blind to the knowledge of God;

Of the holy man, the eyes are open to the knowledge of God; and feathers of light to the world burned.

No one went to the buried treasure of Karun;

And if he found a way, he found not a way out of it.

If thou art a seeker, who over this ground of the knowledge of God dost travel,

First thou shouldst pluck up the foot of the steed of returning;

Shouldst reflect, in the mirror of the mind;

Shouldst acquire purity by degrees.

Possibly the perfume of the love of God makes thee intoxicated;

Makes thee a seeker of the Covenant— "Am I your God?"

With the foot of search thou dost travel to that place;

And thence thou dost fly with the wing of the love of God.

Truth tears the curtains of fancy;

There remains not a lofty curtain, save the glory of God.

Again for the steed of reason there is no running;

Astonishment will seize its rein, saying, "Stand!"

In this sea of God only the man-guardian [Mohammed] went:

That one became lost, who went not behind the inviter [Mohammed].

Those persons who have turned back from this road

Traveled much, and are distressed.

That person who chooses the way opposite to the Prophet

Will never arrive at the stage of his journey.

Oh Sadi! think not that the path of purity

One can travel, except behind the Chosen One.

Generous of dispositions, beautiful of natures!

The Prophet of creatures, the Intercessor of nations!

The Imam of the prophets, the Leader of the road!

The faithful of God, the place of descent of the Angel Jibra'il!

The Intercessor of mortals, the Lord of raising and dispersing!

The Imam of the guides, the Chief of the court of Assembling!

The Speaker, whose Mount Sinai is the celestial sphere;

All lights are the rays of his light.

The orphan who, the Qur'an uncompleted,

Washed the library of so many religions,

When anger drew forth his sword of terror,

Struck, by a miracle, the waist of the moon in two halves.

When his fame fell in the mouths of the people of the world

An earthquake occurred in the court of Kisri.

By the words—*la-ilaha illa-llah* he broke into small pieces the idol Lat;

For the honor of religion he took away the reputation of the idol "Uzzah.

He brought not forth the dust of the idols Lat and 'Uzza only;

But made the Old Testament and Gospel obsolete.

One night he sate on the beast Burak; he passed beyond the Heavens:

In majesty and grandeur he exceeded the angels.

So impetuous, he urged his steed into the plain of propinquity to God,

While Jibra'il remained behind him, at the tree of paradise.

The Chief of the sacred house spoke to him,

Saying: "Oh, bearer of the Divine Revelation! move proudly higher.

"When thou didst find me sincere in friendship,

Why didst thou twist the reins from my love?"

Jibra'il said: "The power to move higher was not to me:

I remained here because the power of wing remained not to me.

If I fly one hair's breadth higher,
The effulgence of splendor will burn my feathers."
On account of sins a person remains not in restraint
Who has such a Lord as guide.
What acceptable praise may I say to thee?
Oh, Prophet of Mortals! peace be on thee!
May the benedictions of angels be on thy soul!
May they be on thy companions and followers!
First Abu-Bakr, the old disciple;
'Umar, grasp on the convolution of the contumacious demon;
The wise 'Usman, night, alive-keeping;
The fourth 'Ali-Shan, Duldul, riding.
Oh God! by the right of the sons of Fatima,
May I, on the word of faith, conclude my life!
If thou dost reject my claim, or if thou dost accept,
I, and the hand, and the skirt of the offspring of the Prophet are together.
Oh chief happy-footed! what loss occurs
Of thy exalted dignity, at the court of the Living One,
That there are a few beggars of the tribe,
Humble companions, guests, at the House of Paradise?
God praised and honored thee, O Mohammed!
Jabra'il performed the ground-kiss of thy worth.
The lofty sky, before thy worth, is ashamed,
Thou created, and man yet water and clay.
Thou from the first, the essence of the existence of man;
Whatever else became existent is an offshoot from thee.
I know not what words I may say to thee,
Who art higher than what I say of thee.
To thee the honor of— "but for thee"—is sufficient grandeur;
Thy praise in the verse of the Koran— "*táhá wa yasin*" — is sufficient.

What praise may the imperfect Sadi make?
Oh Prophet! on thee be benedictions and safety!
In the extremes of the world I wandered much;
With every one I passed my time.
From every corner I found pleasure;
From every harvest I obtained an ear of corn.
Like the pure ones of Shiraz of dust-like disposition,
I saw not one.—May mercy be on this pure soil of Shiraz!
The cultivating of friendship of the men of this pure soil
Drew away my heart from Syria and Turkey.
I said to my heart: "From Egypt they bring sugar;
They take it as a present to friends."
From all that garden or the world I was loath
To go empty-handed to my friends.
If my hand be empty of that sugar,
There are words sweeter than sugar—
Not that sugar that men apparently enjoy;
But that which the lords of truth take away on paper.
May the World-Creator have mercy on thee!
Whatever more I may say is empty talk and wind.

2

# On Justice and Administration of Government

The beneficences of God are not contained in the imagination;

What service does the tongue of praise offer?

Oh God, do thou—this King (Abu-Bakr, son of Sad), the poor man's friend,

Since the ease of the people is in his protection—

Keep long established over the head of the people;

By the grace of devotion, keep his heart alive.

Keep his tree of hope fruitful;

His head green, and his face, with mercy, fair.

Oh Sadi! go not in the way of dissimulation;

If thou hast honesty, bring and come.

Thou art a stage-recognizer, and the King a road traveler:

Thou art a speaker of truth; and the King the hearer of truths.

What necessity that nine thrones of the sky

Thou dost place below the foot of the King Kizil-Arsalan.

Say not: Place thy foot of honor on the Heavens.

Say: Place the face of sincerity in the dust.

Place, in devotion, the face on the threshold of God;

Because this is the highway of the righteous.

If thou (Abu-Bakr) art a slave of God, place thy head on this door of God;

Place from off thy head the cap of lordship.

At the Court of the Order giver possessed of Majesty,

Bewail, like a dervish, before a rich and powerful man.

When thou dost perform thy devotions, put not on the kingly raiment;

Like the poor dervish, bring forth a cry,

Saying: "O Omnipotent One! Thou art powerful;

Thou art strong; Thou art the dervish-cherisher.

"I (Abu-Bakr) am neither a monarch nor an order-giver;

I am one of the beggars of this Court.

"What springs forth from the power of my conduct,

Unless the power of Thy grace is my friend?

"Give to me the means of liberality and goodness;

And if not—what goodness can come from me to any one?

"O God! keep me on the work of goodness;

Otherwise, no work can come from me."

At night, like the beggars, pray with ardor,

If, by day, thou dost exercise sovereignty.

The obstinate ones are at thy door, loin-girt;

Thou shouldst be thus—thy head on the threshold of devotion.

Oh, excellent!—for us slaves, the Lord God;

For the lord a slave, duty-performing.

They relate a story of the great men of the faith,

Recognizer of the truth of the essence of truth,

As follows: A pious man sate on a panther;

Snake in hand, he urged his long, pleasant-paced steed.

One said to him: "Oh, man of the way of God!

Guide me to this road by which thou didst go.

"What didst thou, that the rending animal became obedient to thee?

That the seal-ring of good fortune went to thy name?"

He said: "If the panther and snake be submissive to me,
And if also the elephant and vulture-be not astonished.
"Do thou also from the order of the Ruler twist not thy neck,
So that no one, from thy order, may twist his neck."
When the ruler is obedient to God,
God is his Protector and friend.
It is impossible when He loves thee
That He will leave thee in the power of an enemy.
This is the road, and turn not thy face from the way;
Place thy foot on this road and obtain the object which thou dost desire.
Advice of a person is profitable to a person to him,
To whom the saying of Sadi is agreeable.
I have heard that, at the time of the agony of the soul,
King Naushiravan the Just thus spoke to Hurmuz, his son,
Saying: "Be observant of the heart of the poor;
Be not in the desire of thy own ease.
"A person rests not within thy territory
When thou dost seek thy own ease and no more.
"In the opinion of the wise it is not approved—
The shepherd asleep, and the wolf among the sheep.
"Go: protect the poor and needy one,
Because the king is the crown-holder for the sake of his subjects.
"The subject is like the root, and the king the tree;
Oh son! the tree is strong by reason of the root.
"So long as thou canst, wound not the heart of the people;
But if thou dost—thou dost pluck up thy own roots.
"If a straight road of safety is necessary for thee—
The way of the pious is hope and fear.
"The disposition of man is toward wisdom,
In the hope of goodness, and fear of wickedness."

If thou didst find these two doors in the King,
Thou didst obtain shelter in the territory of his kingdom.
The King brings a gift to the hopeful one,
In hope of the gift of pardon of the Creator of the World.
"The injury of persons is not pleasing to the king,
Who fears lest injury should come to his kingdom.
"And if there is not this disposition in his nature
There is not the perfume of ease in that territory.
"If thou art foot-bound (by wife and family), accept contentment;
But if thou art a single horseman (solitary), take thy own desire.
"Seek not plenteousness in that land and region,
Where thou dost see the subjects of the king sorrowful.
"Fear not the proud, haughty ones;
Fear that one who fears God.
"In a dream, he sees the territory of another populous,
Who keeps the heart of the people of his country distressed.
"From violence come ruin and ill-fame;
The prudent man reaches to the profundity of this speech.
It is not proper with injustice to slay the peasants,
Who are the shelter and support of the kingdom.
"For thy own sake preserve the villagers;
Because the laborer of happy heart executes more work for his master.
"It is not manliness to do ill to that one,
from whom thou mayst have experienced much benefit in tribute."
I have heard that King Khosru said to his son Shirwiya
At that time when his eyes slept from seeing—
"In that state be, so that whatever resolution thou mayst make
Thou mayst consider the peace of the peasant.

"Be sure, so long as thou dost not turn thy head from equity and judgment,

That men will not turn aside their feet from thy power.

"The peasant flies from the tyrant;

He makes his bad repute a stock story in the world.

"Much time passes not, that his own foundation,

That one plucked up, who laid a bad foundation.

"The enemy, skillful with the sword, lays waste,

Not so much as the smoke of the heart of an old woman.

"The lamp of grief that the widow-woman lighted up—

Thou mayst often have seen that it burned a city.

"Who in the world is more favored than that one

Who with justice, in sovereignty, lived?

"When the time of his traveling from this world arrives,

The people of the world send mercy to his tomb.

"Since bad and good men pass away,

It is best indeed that they connect thy name with goodness and bless thee.

"Appoint the God-fearing one over the peasant;

Because, the abstinent one is the architect of the country.

"That liver-eater of the people is thy enemy,

Who seeks thy profit, in the injury of the people.

"Government is a fault in the hands of those persons,

From whose power, the hands of the people are uplifted in prayer before God.

"The cherisher of good sees not evil;

When thou dost cherish evil thou art the enemy of thy own life.

"Exercise not retribution against the despoiler by confiscation of his property;

But it is proper to bring forth to destroy his root from the foundation.

"Exercise not patience with the agent of the friend of tyranny;

Since, on account of his fatness (from extortion), it is proper to flay his skin.

"It is also proper, at first, to cut off the wolf's head,

Not at the time when he tore in pieces the sheep of men."

How well said the captive merchant

When the robbers gathered around him with arrows!—

"Inasmuch as courage comes from highwaymen,

Whether the men of the army, or a troop of women, what matter?"

The great king who injured the merchants

Shut the door of well-being on the people of the city and the army.

How many wise men again go there

When they hear the rumor of bad custom?

Are a good name and favorable reception necessary to thee?—

Hold in esteem merchants and envoys.

Merchants heartily cherish travelers,

Because they carry their good name to the world.

That kingdom soon becomes ruined

From which the injured heart becomes a traveler.

Be the acquaintance of the foreigner, and friend of the traveler,

Because the traveler is one who hawks about a good name.

Hold dear the guest, and precious the traveler;

But also be on guard from injury from them.

To beware of the stranger is good;

Because, possibly, he may be an enemy in the guise of a friend.

Advance the rank of thy own old friends;

Because treachery never comes from the cherished one.

When thy servant becomes old,
Forget not the right of his years.
If old age has bound the hand of his service—-
Yet thou hast power, in respect to liberality.
To accomplish the desire of the hopeful
Is better than to break the bonds of a thousand fettered ones.
If the pillar of the office of the scribe
Balls, he cuts not the rope of hope.
The just monarch, with his subjects,
Becomes angry like a father with a son.
Sometimes he strikes him so that he becomes sorrowful;
Sometimes he makes water flow from his pure eyes.
When thou dost exercise gentleness, the enemy becomes bold;
But if thou art an anvil, he becomes wearied of thee.
Severity and mildness together are best,
Like the vein-striker (bleeder), who is surgeon and plaster placer.
Be generous, and pleasant-tempered, and forgiving;
Even as God scatters favor over thee, do thou scatter over the people.
No one came into the world who remained,
Save that one whose good name remained.
That one aied not, after whom there remained—-
Bridge, or masjid, or khan, or guest-house.
Every one behind whom a token remained not—-
The tree of his existence brought not forth fruit.
If he departed from this world and the marks of his well doing remained not,
It is not fit to chant after his death-— *"Al hamd!"*
When thou dost wish that thy name may be eternal,
Conceal not the good name of the great ones.

After thy own time call to mind that same descriptive picture

That, after the age of former kings, thou didst behold.

One took away a good name from the world;

The bad custom of the other remained behind him forever.

With the ear of approval, listen not to a person's injury;

But if the speech comes, probe its depth.

Accept the excuse of forgetfulness of the sinner;

When he asks for protection, give protection.

If a sinner comes to thy shelter,

It is not proper to slay him at the first fault.

When once they uttered advice, and the sinner heard not;

Punish him, the second time, with imprisonment and bonds.

And if advice and bonds are of no advantage to him,

He is an impure tree; pluck up his roots.

When anger comes to thee, on account of a person's crime,

Reflect much on his punishment;

Because it is easy to break the ruby of Badakhshan.

Broken—it is not possible to fasten it together again.

I heard that King Jamshid, of happy nature,

Wrote on a stone, at a fountain-head:

"At this fountain many like us took rest;

They departed in death, just as the eyes twinkled.

"With manliness and force they took the world;

But they took it not with themselves to the tomb.

"They departed, and each one reaped what he sowed:

There remained only good and bad fame."

When thou hast power over an enemy,

Injure him not; because this is indeed sufficient sorrow to him.

A living enemy, head-revolving about thee in desire of thy blood,

Is better than his life-blood revolving about thy neck.
I heard that Darius, of August family,
Became separated, on a hunting-day, from his retinue;
A herdsman came running toward him:
Darius, of happy sect, said to his heart:
"Perhaps this is an enemy who has come to battle:
From a distance I will pierce him with a white poplar arrow."
He adjusted the royal bow to the bow-string:
He desired in a moment to make his existence non-existence.
The herdsman said: "Oh, Lord of Iran and Turan!—-
May the evil eye be far from thy time!—-
"I am he who cherishes the King's horses;
In this meadow I am in thy service."
The heart of the King, which had gone in fear, returned to its place.
He laughed and said: "O one of contemptible judgment!
"The auspicious angel Jibra'il assisted thee;
Otherwise, I had brought the bow-string to the ear."
The guardian of the land-pastured laughed and said:
"It is not proper to conceal advice from a benefactor;
"It is not laudable deliberation, nor good judgment,
That the King knows not an enemy from a friend.
"The condition of living in greatness is such
That thou shouldst know each humble person—-who he is.
"Thou hast many times seen me in the presence:
Thou hast asked me concerning the herd of horses and the meadow.
"Now in love I returned before thee:
Thou dost not again recognize me from an enemy.
"O renowned monarch! I am powerful;
Because I can bring a particular horse out of a hundred thousand.

"By reason of wisdom and judgment, I have the guardianship of the horses;

Thou also shouldst keep thy own herd permanent."

When Darius heard this counsel from the man

He spoke fairly to him, and did him kindness.

Darius kept going and saying in his shame—

It will be proper to write this advice on the heart.

On account of anarchy there may be sorrow in that throne and country

When the deliberation of the king may be less than that of the shepherd.

How mayst thou hear the lament of one crying for justice-

The curtain of thy bed-place at Saturn?

So sleep that the lamentation may come to thy ear

If the crier for justice brings forth a shout.

Who complains of the tyrant who is in thy time,

When every violence that he commits is thy violence?

The dog tore not the skirt of one of a Karawan,

But the ignorant villager, who cherished the dog.

Oh Sadi! thou camest boldly into speech:

When the sharp sword of true speech is at thy hand, be victorious.

Say what thou dost know; because truth spoken is well:

Thou art not a bribe-taker, nor a blandishment-giver.

Bind avarice to thyself, but then wash the book of philosophy;

Bid farewell to avarice, and say whatever thou dost desire.

A certain neck-exalting one (a king) in Media came to know

That a wretched one beneath an arch kept saying:

"Thou even art hopeful at the door of God:

Then accomplish the hope of those door-sitting."

Thou dost not wish that thy heart may be sorrowful—

Bring forth from fetters the heart of the sorrowing ones.

The distress of the heart of the one justice-seeking
Casts a king from his kingdom.
Thou hast slept cool half a day in the retired place (harem);
Say to the foreigner, burn in the heat outside.
God is the taker of justice for that person
Who can not ask for justice from a king
One of the great ones, possessed of discretion,
Tells a story of the son of King 'Abdu-l-'Aziz,
Saying: he had a ring-stone set in a ring,
In respect to the value of which the Court jeweler was confounded.
At night, thou wouldst say it is the orb, world-illuminating;
A glittering star it was, in light like the day.
By chance a drought-year occurred,
When the full-moon of the face of men became the new-moon.
When he saw not ease and strength in man,
He considered it not manliness to be himself at ease.
When a person sees poison in the jaws of men,
How will the sweet water pass to his throat?
He ordered: they sold the ring-stone for silver
Because pity came to him, on account of the poor and orphan.
He gave its value, in spoil, ill one week:
He gave to the poor, and needy, and necessitous.
Those reproach-making fell on him,
Saying: "Such a ring will not again come to thy hand."
I heard that he said, and the rain of tears
Ran, down, like wax, on his cheeks—
As follows: "Ugly is the ornament on a monarch,
The heart of a citizen afflicted with powerlessness;
"A ring without a stone is fit for me:
The heart of a sorrowful populace is not fit for me."

If a relation of the enemy be friendly to thee,
Beware; be not secure of craftiness.
Because his heart becomes torn for vengeance against thee.
When memory of the love of his own relation comes to him.
Consider not the sweet words of an enemy;
For it is possible there is poison in the honey.
That one took his life safe from the trouble of the enemy
Who reckoned friends as enemies.
That knave preserves the pearl in his purse,
Who considers all people purse-cuts.
The soldier who is an offender against the Amir,
So long as thou canst—-take not into service.
He knew not gratitude toward his own chief;
He knows not thee also: be afraid of his deceit.
Hold him not strong as to oath and covenant;
Appoint a secret watchman over him.
Make long the tether of the aspirant;
Break it not, lest thou shouldst not see him again.
When, in battle and siege, the enemy's country
Thou seizest—-consign it to the prisoners.
Because when a captive plunges his teeth in blood,
He drinks blood from the tyrant's throat.
When thou pluckest away a territory from the enemy's clutch,
Keep the peasantry in more order than he.
For, if he beats open the door of conflict,
The people will pluck out the essence of his brain.
But if thou causest injury to the citizens,
Shut not vainly the city-gate in the enemy's face.
Say not: "The enemy, sword-striking, is at the gate!"
When the enemy's partner is within the city.
Essay with deliberation battle with the enemy;

Reflect on counsel; and conceal thy resolution.

Reveal not the secret to every one;

For I have seen many a cup-sharer a spy.

Sikander, who waged war with the Easterns,

Kept, they say, his tent-door toward the west.

When Bahman wished to go to Zawulistan,

He cast a rumor of his going to the left, and went to the right.

If one, besides thee, knows what thy resolve is—

It is fit to weep over that judgment, and knowledge, and resolution.

Exercise liberality—neither conflict nor rancor—

That thou mayst bring a world beneath thy signet-ring.

When a work prospers through courtesy and pleasantness,

What need of severity and arrogance?

Thou wishest not that thy heart should be sorrowful?

Bring forth from bondage the hearts of those sorrowful.

The army is not powerful by the arm;

Go; ask a blessing from the feeble.

The prayer of the hopeful weak ones

Is of more avail than the manly arm.

Whosoever takes to the dervish his request for aid,

If he strikes at Firidun, he would overcome him.

# 3

## On Beneficence

If thou art wise, incline to truth;
For truth, not the semblance, remains in its place.
To whomsoever there was neither knowledge nor liberality nor piety—
In his form there was no reality.
Beneath the clay sleeps at ease that one
By whom men sleep tranquil at heart.
Suffer thy own grief in life; for the relation,
Through his own avarice, busies not himself with one dead.
Give now gold and silver which is thine;
For after thy death it is out of thy command.
Thou wishest not that thou shouldst be distressed in heart?
Put not out of thy heart those distressed.
Scatter treasures in alms to-day, without delay;
For to-morrow the key is not in thy hand.
Take away with thy self thy own road-provisions;
For compassion after death comes from neither son nor wife.
That one takes away the ball of empire from this world
Who took, with himself, a portion to the future world
With sympathy, like my finger-tip,
No one in the world scratches my back.
Place now, on the palm of the hand, whatever there is;

Lest that, to-morrow (the Judgment-day), thou shouldst with the teeth bite the back of the hand.

Strive as to covering the shame of the dervish,

That the veil of God may be thy secret-concealer.

Turn not the foreigner portionless from thy door,

Lest that thou shouldst become a wanderer in beggary at doors.

The great one causes alms to reach the indigent;

For he fears that he may become necessitous (as to the need of others).

Look into the state of the heart of those wearied;

For thy heart may, perhaps, one day be broken.

Make the hearts of those dejected happy;

Remember the day of helplessness (the Judgment-day).

Thou art not a beggar at the doors of others;

Drive not, in thanks to God, a beggar from thy door.

Cast protection over the head of the one father-dead;

Scatter his dust of affliction, and pluck out his thorn.

Knowest thou not how very dejected his state was?

May a rootless tree be ever green?

When thou seest an orphan, head lowered in front from grief,

Give not a kiss to the face of thy own son.

If the orphan weeps, who buys for his consolation?

And if he becomes angry, who leads him back to quietude?

Beware! that he weep not; for the great throne of God

Keeps trembling when the orphan weeps.

Pluck out with kindness the tear from his pure eye;

Scatter with compassion the dust of affliction from his face.

If his (the father's) protection departed from over his head,

Do thou cherish him with thy own protection.

I esteemed my head crown-worthy at that time

When I held my head in my father's bosom.

If a fly had sate on my body,

The heart of some would have become distressed.

If now enemies should bear me away captive,

None of my friends is a helper.

For me is acquaintance with the sorrows of orphans,

For in childhood my father departed (in death) from my head.

A certain one plucked out a thorn from an orphan's foot;

The Khujand Chief saw him in a dream:

He was talking and sauntering in the gardens of Paradise,

Saying: "How many roses blossomed from that thorn!"

So long as thou canst, be not free from mercy;

For they bear pity to thee, when thou bearest pity.

When thou hast done a favor, be not self-worshiping,

Saying: "I am a superior, and that other an inferior."

Say not: "The sword of Time has cast him!"

For the sword of Time is yet drawn.

When thou seest a thousand persons prayer-uttering for the empire,

Give thanks to God for favors.

For the reason that many men have expectation from thee,

Thou hast expectation at the hand of none.

I have said that liberality is the character of chiefs;

I uttered a mistake—it is the quality of prophets!

I have heard that, one week, a son of the road

Came not to the guest-house of Ibrahim, the friend of God.

Through his happy disposition, he used not to eat in the morning,

Unless one, foodless, came from the path of travel.

He went out, and looked in every direction;

Glanced in the quarters of the valley; and saw:

One, willow-like, in solitude, in the desert;
His head and hair white with the snow of old age.
For consolation he said to him: "Marhaba!"
Uttered, according to the custom of the liberal, the invitation,
Saying: "Oh pupil of my eyes!
Do me a favor, as to bread and salt."
He said, "Yes"; and sprang up and lifted his feet;
For he knew his temperament—on him be peace!
The guards of the guest-house of Ibrahim
Placed the abject old man, with respect.
He ordered; and they arranged the table;
All sate around.
When the company began: *"Bismi-llah!"*
A word from the old man reached not his ear.
He spoke to him, thus: "O old man of ancient days!
I behold not thy truth and heart-burning, like old men.
"When thou eatest food, is it not the custom
That thou shouldst take the name of the Lord of Victuals?"
He said: "I accept not a religion
Which I have not heard from the old men, fire-worshiping."
The prophet of good omen knew
That the old man, of State become ruined, was a Guebre.
He drove him away with contempt when he saw him a stranger to Islam;
For to the pure the filthy is forbidden.
The angel Surosh came from the glorious Omnipotent,
With majesty, reproaching, saying: "Oh, friend of God!
"I had for a hundred years given him victuals and life;
Abhorrence of him comes to thee in a moment.
"If he takes his adoration to the fire,
Why withdrawest thou thy hand of magnanimity?"
I know not who told me this tale,

That there had been, in the country of Yemen, an order-giver.
He snatched the ball of empire from those renowned;
For in treasure-bestowing there was no equal to him.
One could call him "the Cloud of Liberality,"
For his hand used to scatter money like rain.
No one used to take to him the name of Hatim,
At which mentioning, frenzy used not to go to his head,
Saying: "How much—of the words of that wind-weigher,
Who has neither country, nor command, nor treasure?"
I heard that he prepared a royal feast,
And harp-like entertained the people, in the midst of the banquet.
One opened the door of mention of Hatim;
Another began to utter his praise.
Envy held the man to the desire of revenge;
He appointed one for his blood-devouring,
Saying: "So long as Hatim is in my time,
My name will not go into the world for goodness."
The calamity-seeking one took the path to the tribe of Tai,
He set out for the slaying of the young man.
There came before him on the road a young man,
From whom the perfume of affection came up to him:
Good of visage, and wise, and sweet of tongue;
He brought him a guest, that night, to his own abode:
Exercised liberality, and sympathized, and made excuses;
Snatched the enemy's heart by kindness:
Placed the morning-kiss on his hands and feet,
Saying: "Stay at ease, a few days, with us."
He said: "I can not here become a resident;
For I have before me an important matter."
He replied: "If thou wilt reveal the matter to me
I will with soul exert myself, like friends of one heart."

He replied: "Oh young man! listen to me;
For I know the generous one is a secret-concealer.
"Thou knowest, perhaps, in this land, Hatim,
Who is of happy judgment and good manners?
"The King of Yemen has desired his head;
I know not what hatred has arisen between them.
"Show me the short path to where he is;
Oh friend! this indeed I look for from thy courtesy."
The youth laughed, saying: " I am Hatim: Behold!
Separate with the sword the head from my body.
"When the morning becomes white it is not proper that
Injury should reach thee, or that thou shouldst become disappointed."
When Hatim placed, with nobleness, his head for slaughter,
A cry issued from the young man (the guest).
He fell upon the dust, and leaped to his feet;
Kissed now the dust; now his feet and hands:
Threw down the sword, and placed the quiver on the ground;
Put, like the helpless, his hands on his breast,
Saying: "If I strike a rose on thy body,
I am, in men's sight, a woman, not a man."
He kissed both his eyes, and embraced him;
And took his way thence to Yemen.
Between the two eyebrows of the man, the King
Knew immediately that he had not performed the duty.
He said: "Come; what news hast thou?
Why didst thou not bind his head to thy saddle-strap?
"Perhaps a renowned one made an assault against thee;
Thou, through weakness, sustainedst not the fury of the contest?"
The clever youth gave the ground-kiss;
Praised the King; and the majesty of his nature,

Saying: "I discovered Hatim, fame-seeking,
Skillful, and of pleasant appearance, and of good visage:
"Considered him generous and endowed with wisdom;
Regarded him, in manliness, my superior:
"The load of his favor made my back bent;
He slew me with the sword of kindness and grace."
Whatever he experienced, from his liberality-he uttered;
The monarch recited praises on the offspring of Tai:
Gave the envoy gold-money,
Saying "Liberality is the seal on Hatim's name."
It reaches him, if they give evidence;
Since truth and fame are his fellow travelers.

I have heard that in the time of the Prophet the tribe of Tai
Made not acceptance of the faith of the Qur'an.

The Messenger of good news and the Observer (Mohammed) sent an army;
They took captive a multitude of them.

The Prophet ordered them to slay them with the sword of hate,
Saying: "They are unclean, and of impure religion."
A woman said: "I am Hatim's daughter,
Ask pardon for me from this renowned Ruler (Mohammed):
"Oh revered sir! exercise generosity as to my state;
For my lord Hatim was endowed with liberality."
By the command of the Prophet of pure judgment,
They loosed the fetters from her hands and feet:
Drew the sword upon the rest of that tribe,
So that they caused, mercilessly, a torrent of blood to flow.
With weeping the woman said to the swordsman:
"Strike my neck also with all the rest:
"I consider not release from fetters, generosity;

I—alone; and my friends in the noose of calamity."
She kept uttering lamentations over the brothers of Tai;
Her voice came to the Prophet's ear.
The rest of that tribe he gave to her,
Saying: "One of true origin never erred!"
From Hatim's storehouse, an old man
Demanded ten diram's weight of sugar-candy.
From the historian I remember news such
That he sent him a sack of sugar.
The wife said from the tent: "What is this?
The old man's need was exactly ten dirams."
The man-cherisher of Tai heard this speech;
He laughed, and said: "Oh heart's ease of Hai!
"If he demanded what was suitable to his own need, and got it,
Where is the liberality of the offspring of Hatim?"
I have heard that a man experienced house-vexation
For a wasp made a nest in his roof.
His wife said: "What thou desirest in respect to them do not,
Lest that they should become scattered from their native country."
The wise man went to his own work;
The wasps began, one day, to sting his wife.
About the door, and roof, and street—the foolish wife
Kept making lamentation. But the husband said:
"Oh woman! make not thy face bitter toward men;
Thou didst say: 'Slay not the poor wasps!'"
How may one do good to the bad!
Forbearance to ill-doers increases ill.
When thou beholdest a people's injury in a chief,
Cut his throat with a sharp sword.

What dog, in short, is there—for whom they place a victual tray?

Order that they give him a bone.

How well has the old man of the village expressed this proverb:

"The baggage-animal, leg-striking, is best under a heavy load."

If the watchman shows mercy,

No one is able to sleep at night for thieves.

In the circle of contest the spear-reed

Is more precious than a hundred thousand sugar-reeds.

Not every one is worthy of property;

This one requires property; that one, rebuke.

When thou cherishest the cat it takes away the pigeon;

When thou makest the wolf fat it rends Joseph.

The edifice that has not firm foundations—

Make it not lofty; and if thou dost, tremble for it.

How well said Bahram, desert-dwelling,

When his thoroughbred, restive steed threw him to the earth,

"It is proper to take from the herd another horse

Which it is possible to restrain, if he becomes restive."

O son! bind the Euphrates at low-water,

For when the torrent is risen it is of no use.

When the filthy wolf comes to thy snare,

Slay; if not, pluck up thy heart from love for the sheep.

From Iblis adoration never comes;

Nor from the bad jewel-goodness into existence.

Give neither place nor opportunity to the malignant one;

The enemy in the pit, and the demon in the glass bottle is best.

Say not: "It is proper to kill this snake with a stick";

Strike when he has his head beneath thy stone.

The pen striker who did ill to his inferiors,
To make, with the sword, his hand a pen is best.
The deliberator who introduces bad regulations
Takes thee, that he may give thee to hell-fire.
Say not: "For the country this deliberator is enough";
Call him not deliberator who is unfortunate.
The fortunate one acts upon Sadi's speech,

Because it is the cause of increase of country, and deliberation, and judgment.

**4**

# On Love

Oh happy the time of those distraught in love of Him,

Whether they experience the wound (of separation) or the plaster (of propinquity to Him)!

Beggars from royalty fleeing;

In the hope of union with Him, in beggary, long-suffering.

Time to time they drink the wine of pain (of love for Him);

And if they consider it bitter, they draw breath (are patient).

In the pleasure of wine there is the evil of head-sickness;

The thorn is the armor-bearer of the rose-branch.

Patience which is in remembrance of Him is not bitter;

For bitterness from a friend's hand is sugar.

His captive desires not release from bonds;

His prey seeks not freedom from the snare.

Sultans of retirement, beggars of Hai!

Stages of God recognizer, foot-trace lost.

Intoxicated with the love of the friend (God), reproach enduring;

The camel, intoxicated, more easily bears the load.

How may people find the path to their state?

For, like the water of life, they are in darkness.

Like the holy house (Jerusalem) within—full of towers (pomp);

Without-the wall left desolate.

Moth-like, they set fire to themselves;
Silkworm-like, they spin not on themselves a protection.
Mistress in embrace—mistress-seeking;
On the stream-bank, lip dry with thirst.
I say not that as to water they are powerless;
But they are, on the Nile, dropsical.
The love of one, like thyself—of water and clay—
Ravishes patience and heartsease.
In wakefulness—enamored of her cheek and mole;
In sleep—foot-bound, in thought of her.
In truth, thou places thy head at her feet, in such a way
That thou consider the world, in comparison with her existence, non-existent.
When thy gold comes not to the eye (of approval) of thy mistress,
Gold and dust appear to thee the same.
To thee—desire for another appears not;
For with her—place for another remains not.
Thou says: "Her lodging is within my eye";
And if thou closest together the eye— "It is in my heart."
Neither thought of any one, lest thou shouldst become disgraced,
Nor power that thou shouldst, for a moment, become patient.
If she desires thy life, thou places it on the palm of her hand;
And if she puts the sharp sword on thy head, thou places thy head in submission.
When love, whose foundation is on desire,
Is to such a degree tumult-exciting and command-issuing,
Hast thou wonder at the travelers of the path of God
That they should be immersed in the sea of truth—
In passion for the Beloved, with soul engaged;

In remembrance of the Friend (God), careless of the world?

In memory of God, they have fed from the world;

So intoxicated with the splendor of the Cupbearer (God) that they have spilled the wine!

It is impossible to effect their cure with medicine;

For none is acquainted with their pain (of love).

From eternity without beginning, to their ear comes: "Am I not your God?"

With clamor, in a shout, they utter: "Yes!"

A crowd—office-holding, corner-sitting;

Feet clayey, breath fiery—

Pluck up, with a shout, a mountain from its place;

Keep together, with a cry, a city:

Are wind-like, invisible, and swift-moving;

Are stone-like, silent, but praise-uttering.

In the morning, they weep to such a degree that the water

Washes down from their eyes the collyrium of sleep.

Steed of the body slain, with the great austerity with which they have urged the night;

In the morning, shouting, saying: "They are wearied!"

Night and day, in the sea of frenzy and burning;

From perturbation they know not night from day.

So enamored of the splendor of the figure-painter (God)

That they have no occupation with the beauty of the outward form.

The pious ones gave not their hearts to the covering;

And if a fool gave—he is brainless and fleshless.

That one drank the pure wine of the Unity of God,

Who forgot this world and the next.

I have heard that once upon a time one, beggar-born,

Had affection for one king-born.

He went, and cherished a vain desire;

Imagination plunged its teeth in desire.

Mile-stone like, he used not to be free (absent) from his (the prince's) plain;

Bishop-like, at all times, at the side of his horse.

His heart became blood, and the secret remained in his heart;

But his feet, through weeping, remained in the mire of desire.

The guards obtained intelligence of his grief;

They said to him: "Wander not again here!"

A moment, he went; recollection of the friend's face came to him;

Again he pitched his tent, at the head of his friend's street.

A slave broke his head, and hand, and foot,

Saying: "Said we not once to thee-come not here?"

Again to him patience and rest remained not;

On account of his friend's face, patience remained not.

Like flies from off the sugar, with violence him

They used to drive away; but with speed he used to return.

One said to him: "Oh, impudent one of insane appearance!

Thou hast wonderful patience as to blows of stick and stone."

He said: "This violence against me is through his tyranny;

It is not proper to complain of a friend's hand.

"Behold, I express the breath of friendship

If he holds me friend; or, if enemy,

"Expect not, without him, patience from me;

Nay—-even with him, repose has no possibility.

"Neither the power of patience, nor room for anger;

Neither the possibility of being (stopping), nor the foot of flight.

"Say not—-turn aside the head from this door of the court;

Though he place my head, like a tent-peg in the tent-rope.

"Nay—-the moth, life given at its friend's foot,
Is better than alive in its dark corner."
He said: "If thou shouldst suffer the wound of his club?"
He replied: "I will fall at his feet, ball-like."
He said: "If, with the sword, he cuts off thy head?"
He replied: "This much even I grudge not.
"To me—-indeed, there is not so much knowledge-—
Whether the crown or the axe be at my head.
"Display not reproof with me impatient;
For patience appears not in love.
"If my eye becomes white like Yakub,
I abandon not hope of seeing Yusuf.
"One who is happy with another
Is not vexed with him for every little thing."
One day the youth kissed the prince's stirrup;
He became angry; and turned the rein from him.
He laughed, and said: "Turn not the rein;
For the Sultan turns not away the rein from any.
"To me—-by thy existence, existence remains not;
To me—-in memory of thee, self-worshiping remains not.
"If thou observes a crime, reproach me not:
Thou art head brought forth from my collar (of existence)

"I fixed my hand in thy stirrup with that boldness;
For I brought not myself in the account.
"I drew the pen on my own name;
Placed my foot on the head of my own desire.
"The arrow of that intoxicated eye slays me indeed;
What need that thou should bring thy hand to the sword!
"Set fire to the reed, and pass;
So that in the forest neither dry nor green thing may remain."

I have heard that at the chanting of a singer
One of Pari face began to dance.
From the fire of the distracted hearts around her
A candle-flame caught in her skirt.
She became troubled in heart and vexed;
One of her lovers said: "What fear?
"Oh love! as to thee—the fire burned the skirt;
As to me—it burned, all at once, the harvest (of existence)."
If thou art a lover, express not a breath about thyself;
For it is infidelity to speak of lover and one's self.
I recollect hearing from a knowing old man in this way,
That one, distraught with love, turned his head to the desert.
The father, through separation from him, neither ate nor slept;
They reproached the son; he said:
"From that time, when Friend called me one of his own,
Further love for any one remained not to me.
"By God! when He showed me His beauty,
Whatever else I beheld appeared to me fancy."
He who turned away from the people became not lost;
For he found again his own lost one (God).
There are beneath the sky shunners of men,
Whom one can call, at once, wild beast and also angel.
Like the angel, they rest not from remembering the King (God);
Like the wild beast they, night and day, shun men.
Strong of arm (by spirituality); but short of hand (by materiality);
Wise-outwardly mad; sensible-outwardly intoxicated.
Sometimes tranquil in a corner, religious habit-stitching;
Sometimes perplexed in society, religious habit-burning.

Neither passion as to themselves; nor solicitude for any one;

Nor place for any one, in the cell of their unitarianism.

Perturbed of reason, confused of sense;

Ear-stuffed to the word of the adviser.

The duck will not become drowned in the river (of lust);

The samundar! what knows he of the torment of burning?

Empty of hand, men of full stomach (proud);

Desert wanderers, without a Kafila:

They have no expectation of the people's approbation;

For they are approved of God; and that is enough.

Dear ones of God concealed from the people's eye;

Not those waist-cord-possessing, clothed in the habit of the dervish.

They are full of fruit, and shady, vine-like;

Are not like us—of black deeds, and blue garment-dyers.

Head plunged in themselves (in reflection), oyster-like;

Not foam (on mouth) gathered, river-like.

If wisdom be thy friend, be afraid of them (those foam-gathered);

For they are demons in the garb of men.

They are not men indeed of bone and skin;

A true soul is not in every form.

The Sultan (God) is not the purchaser of every slave;

Not beneath every religious garment is there a living man.

If every drop of hail had become a pearl,

The bazaar would have become full of them like small shells.

A person said to a moth: "Oh contemptible one!

Go; take a friend suitable to thyself,

"Go on such a path, that thou mayst see the way of hope;

Thou, and the love of the candle is from where to where?

"Thou art not the samundar; circle not around the fire;
For, manliness is first necessary for man, then conflict.
"The blind mouse (bat) goes hidden from the sun;
For force is foolish against an iron grasp.
"The person whom thou knowest to be thy enemy,
To take for a friend is not the part of wisdom."
No one says to thee: "Thou dost do good
When thou places thy life in the desire of his love.
"The beggar who, of a king, asked (in marriage) for his daughter,
Suffered pushing on the back of his head, and nurtured a vain passion.
"How may she bring into reckoning a lover like thee,
For the faces of kings and sultans are toward her?
"Think not that, in such an assembly, she
Will exercise courtesy to a poor one like thee.
"Or if she practice gentleness toward the whole creation—
Thou art a helpless one—she will exercise severity to thee."
Behold! the ardent moth what it said:
"Oh wonder-displayer! if I burn, what fear?
"Like Ibrahim, a fire of love is in my heart,
That thou mayst consider this candle-dame is to me a rose.
"My heart draws not the skirt of the ravishing one (the candle);
But its love draws the collar of my soul.
"Voluntarily I take not myself to the fire;
But the chain of love is about my neck.
"Even so, I was far, when it burned me;
Not this moment, when the fire of love kindled in me.
"A beloved one, in regard to loveliness, does not do that,
That one can speak to her of continence.
"Who reproaches me for love of the friend,

When, slain at the friend's foot, I am content?
"Knowest thou why I have a lust for destruction,
When it (the candle) is, if I am not-it is proper.
" I will burn because it is the approved beloved,
In whom, the burning of the friend (the moth) makes circulation.
"How long speakest thou to me, saying: "Suitable to thyself
Get a companion, compassionate to thyself"
Nimrod threw Ibrahim, or Abraham, into the fire.
God made the fire a rose-garden for Ibrahim's sake.
"Admonition to that one of distraught state is as if
Thou shouldst say to one scorpion-bitten—lament not!
"Oh, astonished one! utter not advice to that person
In whom thou knowest that it will take no effect.
"To the helpless one, rein-gone from the hand,
They say not: 'O boy! urge slowly.'"
How pleasantly occurred this witticism in the book
Sindbad: "O son! love is fire; advice, wind."
The fierce fire, by the wind, becomes more lofty;
The panther, by striking, becomes more angry.
When I saw, thoroughly thou doest evil
That thou places my face opposite to one like thyself.
Seek one better than thyself, and reckon it gain;
For, with one like thyself, thou loses time.
The self-worshipers go in pursuit of such as themselves;
Those intoxicated of God go in a dangerous street (of love).
When I first possessed desire for this work,
I took up, at once, my heart from desire (of life).
One head-casting is true as a lover;
For one of white-liver is the lover of himself.
Death, in ambush, suddenly slays me;
It is better, indeed, that the delicate one should slay me.

When, doubtless, destruction is written on my head,
Destruction is most pleasant by the hand of the beloved.
Dost thou not, one day, in helplessness, yield the soul?
Then it is best thou surrender it at the feet of the beloved.
One night I recollect that my eyes slept not;
I heard that a moth spoke to a candle,
Saying: "I am a lover; if I burn, it is lawful,
Wherefore is thy weeping and burning?"
It replied: "Oh, my poor lover!
Honey (wax), my sweet friend, has departed from me.
"When sweetness (wax) goes away from me,
Like (the statuary) Farhad, fire goes to my head."
The candle kept speaking—and every moment a torrent of grief
Ran down on its yellow cheeks—
Saying: "Oh claimant! love is not thy business;
For thou hast neither patience nor the power of standing.
"Thou dost fly from before a naked flame;
I am standing until I completely burn.
"If the fire of love burns my feathers,
Behold me, whom it burns from head to foot.
"Observe not my splendor, assembly-illuminating;
Consider the heat and torrent of my heart-burning.
"Like Sadi, whose outward form is illuminated;
But, if thou look, his vitals are burned."
A portion of the night, even so, had not passed,
When one of Pari-face suddenly extinguished it.
While its smoke rose to its head, it kept saying:
"Oh, son! this is indeed the end of love!"
This is the way of God, if thou wilt learn;
By being slain, thou wilt obtain ease from the burning (of love)

Make not lamentation over the grave of one slain by the friend;

Say: "Praise be to God! that he is accepted by Him."

If thou art a lover, wash not the hand of sickness (of love).

Wash the hand, like Sadi, of worldly design.

The one who sacrifices his life keeps not his hand from his object,

Though they rain arrow and stone on his head.

I said to thee, "Beware; go not to the ocean;

But if thou goest, entrust thy body to the storm."

5

## On Contentment

He knew not God and worshiped not,

Who displayed not contentment with his fortune and daily food.

Contentment makes a man rich;

Inform the greedy one, world-traveling:

Oh, one without permanence! bring tranquillity to thy hand.

For vegetation grows not on the rolling stone.

If thou art a man of judgment and sense, cherish not thy body;

For when thou cherishest it, thou slayest it.

Wise men are skill-cherishers;

But body-cherishers are feeble in skill.

Eating and sleeping is the way of beasts alone;

To be in this way is the habit of the unwise.

That one attended to a manly life

Who silenced first the dogs of lust.

Happy that fortunate one who, in a corner,

Gathers to his hand road-provisions of the knowledge of God.

Those to whom God's mystery became revealed

Preferred not the false to it.

But when he knows not darkness from light,

Whether the sight of a demon, or the cheek of a houri-to him what difference?

Thou didst cast thyself into a well, on that account,
That thou didst not recognize the well from the road.
How may the young hawk fly to the zenith of the sky
When, in its long feathers, the stone of desire is bound?
If from lust's claw, thy skirt free
Thou shouldst make, thou wouldst go to the lotus-tree.
By eating less food than one's custom,
One can make the body of angelic temperament.
How may the brutal lion reach the angel state?
It can not fly from earth to sky.
Practice first the human temperament;
Think after that of the angelic temperament.
Thou art on the flanks of a refractory colt;
Take care that it twist not its head from thy order.
For if it should tear the halter from thy hand,
It would slay thy body and spill thy blood.
If thou art a man, eat food within limit;
Such a full belly!—art thou a man, or a jar?
Within the body is a place for food, and reflection on God, and breath;
Thou thinkest it is for bread only.
In the wallet of lust, where is remembrance of God contained?
With difficulty he breathes—leg extended.
The body-cherishers have no knowledge
That the full stomach is void of wisdom.
The two eyes and stomach became not filled with anything;
These bowels, coil on coil, are best empty.
Like hell which they fill with fuel,
Again there is a shout, saying: "Is there any more?"
Thy 'Isa (the soul) continually dies of weakness;
Thou art in that desire that thou mayst cherish thy ass (the body) .

Oh, one of little worth! buy not the world in exchange for religion;

Purchase not thou the ass with the gospel of 'Isa.

Perhaps thou seest not that as to rapacious and non-rapacious animals,

Only the greed of eating casts into the snare.

The panther, which stretches its neck (in pride) among the beasts,

Falls, mouse-like, into the snare, through the greed of eating.

Mouse-like, whose bread and cheese thou eatest,

Into his snare thou fallest and sufferest his arrow.

If food be delicious, or if it be simple,

When delay occurs to thy hand, thou eatest pleasantly.

The sage places his head on the pillow at that time when

Sleep takes him, with violence, into its net.

So long as thou obtainest not the power of speech, speak not;

When thou seest not the plain (of power), beware of the ball (of speech).

Speak not; and so long as thou canst, plant not thy foot

Outside of limit, or inside of limit.

Go; acquire a pure heart;

The belly will not become full, save with the dust of the grave.

A Hadji gave me an ivory comb,

Saying: "May the mercy of God be on the good qualities of pilgrims!"

I heard that once upon a time he had called me a dog,

For his heart was, in some way, dejected about me.

I threw away the comb, saying: "This bone,

Is unnecessary for me; another time, call me not a dog.

" Think not, if I swallow my own vinegar,

That I will endure the violence of the lord of sweetmeats."

O soul! be content with a little

That thou mayst consider the sultan and the dervish as one.

Why goest thou before the king with entreaty ?

When thou places avarice aside, thou art a king.

And if thou art a self-worshiper, make the belly a drum;

Make the door of this and that man a Kibla.

And if every moment thy lust says, give!

It causes thee to wander, village to village, in beggary.

Oh, man of sense, contentment exalts the head;

The head full of avarice comes not forth from the shoulder.

A certain one possessed of avarice, before King Khwarazm

I heard—-went early in the morning.

When he saw Khwarazm he became doubled and straight;

He rubbed his face, moreover, on the earth, and arose.

His son said: "Oh little father, name-seeking!

I ask of thee a difficulty; explain it.

"Didst thou not say that the dust of Hijaz was thy Kibla?

Why didst thou to-day pray in this direction?

Display not devotion to the lust of the lust-worshiper;

Since it has every hour another Kibla.

Avarice spilled the reputation of honor;

It poured out a skirt full of pearls for two barley-grains.

When thou wishest to become satiated with the rivulet-water,

Why spillest thou face-water (honor) for the sake of ice?

Perhaps thou art a patient one as to happiness;

But if not thou art, of necessity, begging at doors.

Sir! go; make short the hand of avarice;

What need to thee of the long sleeve of beggary?

Of him who folded up the casket of avarice

It is unnecessary to write: "Slave or servant to any one."

Expectation will drive thee from every assembly;

Drive it from thyself, so that no one may drive thee.

To one of the holy men a fever came,

A person said: "Ask for sugar from such a one."

He said: "Oh, son! the bitterness of my dying

Is better than my bearing the oppression of one of bitter face."

The wise man ate not sugar from the hand of that one

Who, through arrogance, made his face vinegar (bitter) toward him.

Go not in pursuit of whatever thy heart desires,

For the strengthening of the body diminishes the soul's light.

Imperious lust makes a man contemptible;

If thou art wise, hold it not dear.

If thou enjoyest whatever may be thy wish,

Thou wilt endure much disappointment from the revolution of time.

To heat constantly the oven of the belly

May, in the day of want, be a misfortune.

In straitened circumstances thy face causes not its complexion to be shed

If, in the time of plenteousness, thou makst the belly tight.

The man, full-devourer, endures the belly load;

And if he obtain not food, he endures the grief-load.

Thou mayst often see the belly-slave greatly ashamed,

In my opinion the belly straitened is better than the heart straitened.

Alas! thou art one man-born, full of dignity,

Who is like the beasts— "Nay; they are lost!"

Show not pity to the ox of great weight,

For it is a great sleeper and great devourer.

If fatness, ox-like, be necessary to thee,
Submit thy body, ass-like, to the tyranny of persons.
Knowest thou what wonderful thing I brought from Basra?—

A tale, which is sweeter than the green date.
We—a few individuals in the religious garb of the true—

Passed by the side of a date-garden.
One among us was a glutton;
He was, through this narrow-eyedness a belly-enjoyer.
The wretched one bound his loins and ascended the date-tree;
And thence fell heavily headlong.
The Ra'is of the village came, saying: "Who slew this man"
I said: "Express not against us a harsh word.
"The belly drew his skirt down from the branch."
The one of narrow heart is of capacious bowels.
Not every time can one eat the date and carry it away;
The stomach-barn (the glutton) suffered a bad end, and died.
The belly is the hand-fetter and foot-chain;
A belly-slave rarely worships God.
The locust is assuredly altogether belly;
The ant of small belly drags the locust by the foot.
A certain one had sugar-cane, on a small plate—
A wanderer, left and right, for a purchaser.
In a corner of the village, to a pious man, he spoke,
Saying: "Take; and pay when thou hast the means."
That wise man of adorned disposition uttered
An answer, that should be written on the eye.
"Perhaps, to thee, patience (as to payment) may not be exercised toward me;

But to me patience is as to the sugar-cane."
Sugar in its reed has no sweetness
When behind it is the bitter demand for its price.
To one of the men of illumined mind
The Amir of Shutan gave a piece of silk cloth.
He expanded, through gladness, like the laughing rose-leaf;
Kissed his hands, clothed himself, and said:
"How good is the garment of honor of the King of Khutan!
But my own religious garment is more beautiful than it."
If thou art noble, sleep on the earth; for it is enough;
Perform no one's ground-kiss for a costly carpet.
A certain one had no bread-food, save an onion;
He had no resources and means, like others.
One said to him: "Oh, one of foolish time!
Go; bring something cooked from the tray of plunder (the king's table).
"Oh sir! ask, and have fear of none;
For the one ashamed is cut as to his victuals."
He bound about him his overcoat, and quickly folded his hand;
They rent his coat, and broke his hand.
I have heard that he said, while he wept blood:
"What is the remedy for the deed done by one's self!
"The captive of avarice is one calamity-seeking,
After this—I and my house, bread and onion are enough."
The barley-loaf, which I eat by the power of my arm,
Is better than flour twice sifted on the tray of people of liberality.
Last night how heart-straitened slept that worthless one
Who kept the ear of expectation upon the Kibla of others!
In an old woman's house there was a certain cat
Which was of reversed fortune and of bad state.

It went running to the Amir's guest-house;
The slaves of the sultan struck it with arrows.
It ran, blood dropping from its bones (wounds),
While from fear of life it ran, it kept saying:
"If I escape from the hand of this arrow-caster,
I and the mouse and the old woman's desolate abode are enough."
Oh, my soul! honey is not worth the sting's wound;
Contentment with one's own syrup of dates is best.
The Lord God is not satisfied with that slave
Who is not content with his Lord's portion.

# 6

# On Education

The language of this chapter is on integrity, and deliberation, and disposition;

Not on the steed, and the battle-field, and the ball-game.

Thou art fellow-lodger with the enemy-lust;

Why art thou a stranger in the art of conflict?

Those turning back the rein of lust from forbidden things

Surpassed Rustem and Sam in manliness.

Chastise thyself with a stick, boy-like;

Beat not men's brains with the heavy mace.

No one has concern for an enemy like thee

Who prevailest not against thy own body.

Thy body is a city full of good and bad;

Thou art sultan; and wisdom is the prime minister.

Know for sure that the mean, neck-exalting,

In this city are-pride and passion and avarice.

Resignation and the fear of God are the free of good report;

Bust and concupiscence are highwaymen and cut-purses.

When the sultan displays favor to the bad,

How may ease remain for the wise?

Lust and avarice and pride and envy

Are like blood in thy veins; and like the soul in thy body.

If these enemies should obtain nurture,

They would turn aside their heads from thy order and judgment.

On the part of lust and concupiscence, opposition remains not

When they experience the grasp of sharp wisdom.

The Ra'is who punished not the enemy

Ruled not also—-by reason of the enemy's power.

What need to say much in this chapter

When a word is enough, if a person acts upon it?

If thou bringest thy feet mountain-like (firmly) beneath thy skirt,

Thy head will pass beyond the sky in grandeur.

There was a young man, skillful and learned,

Who was, as regards admonishing, vigilant and manly.

Of good repute, and pious, and God-worshiping,

The beard of his face more beautiful than his handwriting.

Strong in eloquence, and clever in grammar;

But he used not to utter truly the letters of the Abjad.

Perhaps he had stammering in the tongue,

For he used not to explain the truth of the Mu'jam.

I spoke to one of the pious,

Saying: "A certain one has no front teeth."

At my folly he became red of face

Saying: "Speak not again in this foolish way.

"Thou didst see in him that very defect which is existent;

From how much skill thy wisdom's eye was shut!

"Listen truly to me; for in the day of certainty (Resurrection),

The man, good-seeing, will not experience evil.

"One who has grace, and science, and judgment-—

If the foot of his integrity slips from its place.—

"Approve not violence against him, for one small matter.

What have the sages said: Take what is clean."

Oh wise man! the thorn and the rose are together:

Why art thou in the fetter of the thorn? fasten thou the rose-bouquet.

He in whose nature is the ugly disposition

Sees not the peacock—only his ugly foot.

O one of malevolent face! acquire purity of heart;

For the dark mirror displays not the face.

Seek a path by which thou mayst escape from punishment of hell;

Not a word of man, on which thou mayst lay the finger of criticism.

O wise one! place not in front (expose not) the people's defects;

For it sews up thy eyes from thy own defects.

Why do I inflict punishment on the one of stained skirt

When I know, within myself, that I am of wet (stained) skirt?

It is improper that thou shouldst exercise violence against a person

When thou dost aid thyself by artifice of speech.

When evil is unpleasant to thee, do not do it thyself;

Say, after that, to thy neighbor: "Do not evil."

If I am God-worshiping, or if self-displaying,

I preserve my exterior for thee, my interior for God.

When I adorned my exterior with chastity,

Interfere not with my crookedness, or uprightness.

If my way of life be good, or if bad,

God is more acquainted than thou with my secret.

Punish for bad conduct that person

Who hopes from thee the reward of goodness.

If I am good or bad, be thou silent;

For I am myself the porter of profit and loss.

For a good deed by a man of good judgment—

For one, God writes ten.

O son! of whomsoever thou also a single talent
Mayst observe, pass by his ten defects.
Count not upon the finger one defect of his;
Bring forth a world of excellence for nothing
Like the enemy, who, on the poetry of Sadi,
Glances with scorn, heart ruined—
He has no ear for the hundred beautiful subtleties;
When he beholds a defect, he raises a shout.
That one, bad-approving—to whom there is only this reason—
Envy plucked out his eyes, good-discerning.
Did not God's creating create the people?
Black, and white, and beautiful, and ugly-came.
Not every eye nor eyebrow that thou seest is good;
Eat the kernel of the pistachio-nut; cast away its husk.

## THANKS

I can not express a breath for thanks to my Friend (God);
For I know not a word of praise that is worthy of Him.
Every hair on my body is a gift from Him;
How may I perform thanks for every hair?
Praise to the Lord-Giver
Who, from nonentity, made the slave existing.
To whom is there the power of description of His beneficence?
For His praises are immersed in His dignity.
That inventor who creates a person from clay
Gives soul and wisdom and sense and heart.
From the father's back-bone to the limit of old age,
Behold to what extent He, from the unseen, gave thee honor!
When God created thee pure, be sensible and pure;
For it is a shame to go unclean to the dust of the grave.

Shake off continually the dust of mean qualities from the mirror of the heart;

For it takes not polish when the blight eats it.

In the beginning, wast thou not water of man's seed?

If thou art a man, put presumption out of thy head.

When thou bringest, with effort, victuals to thyself,

Rely not on the strength of thy own arm.

Oh self-worshiper! why dost thou not see God

Who brings into revolution the arm of the hand?

When by thy striving, a thing happens,

Know by God's grace it is; not by thy own effort.

By violence no one has carried off the ball;

Utter praise to the Lord of Grace.

Of thyself, thou art not erect one step;

From the hidden, aid arrives momently.

Wast thou not a child, tongue-bound as to boast (of speech)?

Food from the navel kept coming within thee.

When they severed the umbilical cord, thy daily food was broken off;

Thy hand clung to thy mother's breast.

A traveler, before whom adverse time brings sickness,

They give to him water from his own city, as medicine.

Then he obtained nourishment in the belly;

He obtained food from the store of the bowels.

The two breasts—that to-day are heart-pleasing to him—

Are also two fountains of his nurturing-place.

The bosom and breast of the mother, heart-pleasing,

Are paradise; and the breast is for him a stream of milk.

Her stature, life-nourishing, is a tree;

The offspring on her bosom—a delicate fruit.

Are not the veins of the breast within the heart?

Then if thou wilt consider, milk is the heart's blood.

Teeth, sting-like, plunged in her blood;

Love for her own blood-devourer created within her.

When God made the arm strong; and the teeth dense—

The nurse anoints her breast with aloes.

The aloe makes it (the offspring) silent (forgetful) of milk, so

That it forgets the breast and its milk.

Oh sir! thou also art, as to repentance, a child of the path of God;

By bitterness, sin becomes forgotten by thee.

A young man turned his head from his mother's judgment,

Her sorrowful heart burned like fire.

When she became helpless she brought a cradle before him,

Saying: "Oh, one languid of love and forgetful of the time of infancy!

"Wast thou not weeping, and tired and small,

When nights, from thy power, sleep overpowered me not?

"No; to thee in the cradle there was not the strength of thy present state;

To thee there was not the power to drive away a fly from thyself.

"Thou art that one who used to be vexed with a single fly,

Who, to-day, art chief and powerful."

Thou mayst again be in that state, at the bottom of the grave,

When thou canst not repel an ant from thy body.

Again how may the eye light up its lamp,

When the worm of the grave devours the fat of the brain?

Like one clothed as to the eye (blind), seest thou not that the road

He knows not, at the time of going, from the well?

Thou who art possessed of vision, if thou didst perform thanks (knowest the path from the well);

If not, thou also art one clothed as to the eye (blind).

The instructor taught thee not understanding and judgment;

God created these qualities in thy existence.

If He had refused thee a heart, truth-hearing,

Truth would have appeared to thy eye the essence of falsehood.

Behold one finger, with how many joints,

God, by creating, cast together.

Then it is madness and foolishness

That thou shouldst place thy finger on the word of His creating.

For the sake of man's motion consider

Him who fixed the sinews and placed the articulations of so many bones.

For without the revolution of the ankle, and the knee, and the foot,

It is impossible to raise the foot from its place.

Prostration is not difficult for a man, on that account,

That, the joint in his back-bone is not of one piece.

God has arranged two hundred joints within one another,

Who has finished like thee, oh, God! a clay-joint?

Oh, one of agreeable disposition! the veins in thy body

Are a land—in it are three hundred and sixty streams.

In the head-vision, and thought, and judgment, and discretion;

The limb of the body for the dear heart; and the heart for dear wisdom.

The wild beasts with the countenance downcast, are contemptible;

Thou, *Alif*-like, art a rider on thy feet.

They, head-lowered, for the sake of eating;

Thou, with dignity, bringest thy food to the head.

It beseems thee not, with so much chieftainship,

That thou shouldst lower thy head, save in devotion to God.

By His own beauty God gave thee knowledge; behold!

He made thee not, like the animals, head in the grass.

But with this form, heart-enchanting,

Be not fascinated; take a good walk of life.

A straight path is necessary, not erect stature;

For the infidel is also like us in outward form.

He who gave thee eye and mouth and ear;

If thou art wise-strive not in opposition to Him.

I grant that thou mayst beat the enemy with a stone,

Wage not war, at least from ignorance, with the Friend (God).

Those of wise disposition, obligation-recognizing,

Sew up the favor of God with the nail of thanks.

A certain one severely rubbed a boy's ears (chastised him),

Saying: "Oh father of wonderful judgment, of overturned fortune!

"I gave thee an axe, saying: Split firewood;

I said not: Undermine the masjid-wall!"

The tongue came from God for thanks and praise;

The grateful one moves it not in slander.

The ear is the thoroughfare for the Koran and counsel;

Strive not to listen to calumny and falsehood.

Two eyes, for the sake of beholding the creating of God, are good;

Lower the eyes from the defect of brother and friend.

For the sake of thy ease the night and day are;

The resplendent moon and the sun, world-illuminating.

For thy sake the west wind, chamberlain-like,

Causes constantly to be spread the carpet of spring.

If wind, and snow, and rain, and hail are,

And if the Chaugan expresses thunder, and the sword lightning—

All are work-performers, and order-bearers of God
Who cherish thy seed in the dust.
And if thou remainest thirsty, rage not through affliction; for the
Water-carrier brings thee a cloud of water on His back.
From the dust He brings color, and perfume, and food;
Amusement for the eye, and brain, and palate.
He gave thee honey from the bees, and manna from the sky;
He gave thee the green date from the date-tree, and the date tree from the seed-stone.
All the gardeners gnaw the hand
In astonishment, saying: "No one planted such a date-tree!"
The sun and moon and Pleiades, all are for thee;
They are the candles of the roof of thy house.
He brings thee a rose from the thorn, musk from the animal's navel,
Gold from the mine, and the green leaf from the dry wood.
He portrayed thy eye and eyebrow, with His own hand;
For one can not leave the intimate friend to strangers.
The powerful One who cherishes the delicate
Cherishes thee with various favors.
Breath by breath, with soul, it is proper to utter praise;
For thanks to Him is not a work of the tongue only.
O God! my heart became blood, and eye wounded,
When I see thy reward is greater than my speech of thanksgiving.
I speak not of the rapacious and non-rapacious beast, and ant, and fish,
But of the army of angels above heaven's summit.
Yet they have uttered a little Thy praise;
They have uttered one out of so many thousands which they should have uttered.
Oh Sadi! go; wash thy hand, and the book;

Hasten not on the path that has no end.
A person knows not the value of a day of pleasure,
Save on that day when he falls to hardship-enduring
The winter-season of the dervish, in the narrow year—
How easy is it to the lord of wealth?
One healthy who, once complaining, slept not,
Uttered not thanks to God for sound health.
When thou art a manly mover, and swift of foot,
Stand, with thanks to God by those slow of foot.
The young man bestows to the ancient old man;
The powerful one displays pity for the powerless.
What do the people of the Jihun know of the value of water?—
Ask those wearied utterly in the sun.
To the Arab who is sitting by the Tigris
What care is there as to the thirsty ones of the desert of Zarud?
That one recognized the value of healthiness
Who once helpless sweltered in fever.
How may the dark night appear long to thee
Who rollest from side to side in comfort?
Think of one falling and rising in fever;
For the sick one knows the lengthiness of the night.
At the sound of the drum the rich man becomes awake;
What knows he how the watchman passed the night?
I have heard that Tughril, one night in the autumn,
Passed a Hindu watchman,
From the pouring of snow, and rain, and torrent,
Fallen to trembling, like the star Canopus.
His heart, from pity for him, suffered agitation;
He said: "Behold! put on my fur garment.
"Wait a moment, by the terrace-side;

For I will send it out by the hand of a slave."
He was in this speech; and the morning-breeze blew.
The monarch entered the royal hall.
He had in his retinue a slave of Pari-form
For whom his disposition had a little inclination.
The sight of the beloved chanced so agreeably to him
That the wretched Hindu passed from his memory.
The word "fur-coat" passed to his (the watchman's) ear,
It came not, through misfortune, to his shoulders.
Perhaps the torment of toil was not enough for him,
Since the sky's revolution added to it expectation.
When the sultan slept in carelessness, behold
What the watchman said to him in the morning!
"Perhaps the watchman Nek-Bakht was forgotten by thee
When thy hand went to the bosom of the slave-girl Aghosh.
"For thee, the night passes in ease and joy;
As to us, what knowest thou how the night passes?"
One of a caravan, head-lowered to the caldron—
To him, what care of those sunk in sand?
Oh Lord of the Zaurak! keep on the water;
For the water has passed over the head of those helpless.
Oh, vigorous young men! stay;
For in the caravan are sluggish old men.
Thou hast slept well in the *haudaj* of the caravan—
The camel-rein in the camel-driver's hand.
Whether plain or mountain; whether stone or sand—to thee what matter?
Ask the state of the road from those lagging behind.
The camel of burden, mountain-form, carries thee;
What knowest thou of the footman, who devours the blood of grief?
Those sleeping in comfort of heart in the house,

What know they of the state of the hungry belly?
One of naked body made loan of one diram;
He made for his body a garment of rawhide.
He complained, saying: "Oh, perverse fortune!
I am cooked with heat, within this rawhide."
When the uncooked (foolish) one, with fierceness, began to boil-—
One from the prison-pit said to him: "Silence!
"Oh raw one! offer thanks to God,
That thou art not like me—-rawhide (bound) on hand and foot."
A certain one passed by a holy man,
He came to his sight in the form of a Jew.
He struck him a blow on his neck;
The dervish gave him his shirt.
He became ashamed saying: "What passed from me was a fault.
Pardon me; what room is there for giving a shirt?"
He said: "On this shirt-giving I am firm, in thanks to God,
That that one whom thou didst think me, I am not."
One left behind on the road was weeping, Saying:
"Than I in this desert, who is more wretched?"
An ass, load-carrier, said to him: "Oh, one without discretion!
How long bewailest thou also of the tyranny of the heavens?
"Go; thank God although thou art not on an ass,
That thou art, in short, a son of Adam, not an ass."
A lawyer passed by one fallen drunk;
He became proud of his own abstinence.
Through haughtiness he looked not at him;
The young man raised his head, saying: "Oh, old man!
"Go; thank God, when thou art in prosperity,
For disappointment comes from pride.

"Laugh not at one whom thou seest in bonds;
Lest that suddenly thou shouldst fall into confinement.
"In short, is it not in the possibility of fate
That thou mayst be to-morrow fallen drunk like me?"

**REPENTANCE**

Oh, thou whose age has passed to seventy years! Come;
Thou wast, perhaps, asleep, that thy life went to the wind.
Thou didst prepare every requisite of being in this world;
Didst not engage thyself in the thought of going to the next world?
On the Resurrection-day, when they lay out the market of heaven,
They give dignities for good deeds.
Stock in trade, as much as thou bringest thou takest away;
And if thou art poor, thou takest away shame.
For the more full the market, just so much
The more distressed is the heart of the one of empty hand.
If out of fifty dirams five become wanting,
Thy heart, with the grasp of grief, becomes torn.
When fifty years have gone forth from thy hand,
Consider it gain that there is a space of five days.
If the wretched corpse had possessed a tongue
He would have raised a shout in lament and cry,
Saying: "Oh living one! when there is the power of speech
Let not the lip sleep, corpse-like, from uttering the name of God.
"Since our time, in carelessness passed,
Do thou, at least, reckon a few moments-opportunity."
One night, in youth and the pleasure of affluence (of youth),
We, young men, sate sometime together.
Nightingale-like, singing; rose-like, fresh of face;
From hilarity, clamor cast into the street.

An old man, world-experienced, apart from us,
The blackness of his hair white, through the violence of Time,
Was tongue-bound, as to speech, nut-like;
Was unlike us, lip from laughter, pistachio-nut-like.
A youth went before him, saying: "Oh, old man!
Why sittest thou with sorrow in the corner of regret?
"Raise once thy head from the collar of grief;
Move jauntily, with ease of heart, with the young men."
He year-stricken raised his head from concealment;
Behold his answer! how like an old man he spoke:
"When the morning breeze blows over the garden
It befits the young tree to move to and fro.
"The green corn, so long as it is young and the head green, waves;
When it reaches mellowness it becomes broken.
"In the spring-time, when the wind brings the fragrance of the musk-willow,
The ancient tree sheds its dry leaves.
"It does not beseem me to move jauntily with young men
When the morning of old age has blossomed on my cheek.
"The male falcon of my soul, which was within my bonds,
Wishes, from time to time, to snatch the end of the thread of life.
"Yours is the time to sit at this tray of enjoyment;
For we have washed our hands of luxurious enjoyment.
"When the dust of venerability sits on the head,
Look not again for the pleasure of youth.
"Snow rained on my raven feathers (hair),
The spectacle of the garden, nightingale-like, is not suitable to me.
"The peacock, possessed of beauty, makes display;
What desirest thou of the hawk, feather-stripped?

"For me, the reaping of the corn is near;
For you, now the fresh verdure of the beard grows.
"The freshness of our rose-garden has passed;
Who binds the rose-bouquet when it has become withered?
"Oh, soul of father! my reliance is on a staff;
Further reliance on life is a mistake.
"For the young man it is reserved to leap on his feet;
For old men prefer a request for aid to the hands of others.
"Behold the red rose of my face-pure yellow;
When the sun becomes yellow it descends.
"To entertain lust, on the part of an immature youth,
Is not so odious as on the part of an old man.
"It is proper for me to weep, like children,
For shame of my sins; not to live, childlike in sport."
Lokman spoke well saying: "Not to live
Is better than to live years in sin."
Even to shut the shop-door in the morning
Is better than to give from the hand the profit and capital of life.
While the young man causes the blackness (of hair) to attain to light (whiteness),
The wretched old man takes his whiteness to the grave.
Oh bone-cage! knowest thou
That thy soul is a bird; and its name spirit?
When the bird departs from the cage of the body, and snaps its chain,
It becomes not, by effort, again thy prey.
Take care of opportunity; for the world is for a moment;
In the opinion of the wise, a moment of life is better than a world.
Sikandar, who held sway over a world,
Abandoned the world, at that time when he died.

To him it was unattainable that—a world from him
They might take; and give him, in return, a moment's respite.
They departed, and every one reaped what he sowed;
There only remains—good and bad name.
Why place we the heart on this caravan-place,
From which friends have departed; and we are on the road?
After us—the garden gives this very rose;
Friends sit with one another.
Fix not the heart on this mistress of the world;
For she sate with no one whose heart she ravished not.
I remember, in my father's time—
The rain of mercy, every moment on him!—
That he purchased in my childhood a tablet and book;
He bought for my sake also a gold ring
Suddenly a purchaser took off
The ring from my hand for a single date.
When the little boy understands not the value of a ring,
They can take it away from him for a sweetmeat.
Thou also didst not recognize life's value
When thou didst throw it away for sweet ease.
On the Resurrection-day, when the good attain to the highest dignity,
They rise from the bottom of the grave—ashes to the Pleiades.
Thy head will, from shame, remain lowered before thee,
When thy bad deeds arise around thee.
Brother! have shame of the work of the bad;
For thou wilt become ashamed in the presence of the good.
On that day, when they ask of thy deeds and words,
The body of the lords of resolution (the prophets) will tremble from fear.

In the place where the prophets suffer fear,

Come, what excuse for sin, hast thou?

**ON PRAYER**

Come; let us raise a hand from the heart;

For to-morrow (after death), one can not raise the hand from the clay of the grave.

In the autumn season, seest thou not the tree

Which, from severe cold, remains leafless!

It uplifts the empty hands of supplication.

It returns not, through God's mercy, empty-handed (leafless).

Fate gives to it a renowned dress of honor;

Destiny places fruit within its bosom.

At that door, which God never closed—think not

That he, hands raised in supplication, becomes hopeless.

All bring devotion; and the wretched, supplication;

Come, so that at the Court of the Cherisher of the Wretched (God)

We may raise the hand, like the naked (leafless) branch;

For one can not sit longer than this without means (leafless).

Oh Lord! look with bounty

When sin comes into existence (issues) from Thy slaves.

Sin issues from the dust-like slave,

In hope of the pardon of the Lord.

O Merciful One! we are cherished by Thy bounty;

We are accustomed to Thy favor and grace.

When a beggar experiences liberality, and grace, and tenderness,

He turns not back from the rear of the giver.

Since Thou didst make us precious in the world,

We have expectation of this same dearness in the future world.

Thou alone givest preciousness and despicability;
One dear to Thee experiences contempt from none.
O God! by Thy honor, make me not contemptible in the future world;
By the baseness of sin, make me not ashamed.
Make not a person like unto myself ruler over me;
If I bear punishment it is best from Thy hand.
There is no evil in the world worse than this—
To suffer oppression from the hand of one like unto myself.
Shame of Thee is for me enough;
Make me not further ashamed before any.
If a shadow from Thee falls on my head,
For me the sky is of the lowest rank.
If Thou grantest a crown, it exalts my head;
Raise Thou me, so that none may cast me down.
My body trembles when I bring to recollection
The prayers of one distraught, in the sacred enclosure at Mecca,
Who, with much lamentation, was saying to God:
"Cast me not away; for no one takes my hand.
"Call me with kindness to Thy door; or drive me from Thy door—
My head is only at Thy threshold.
"If Thou knowest that we are wretched and helpless;
We are wearied of imperious lust.
"This headstrong lust hastens to such a degree
That reason can not seize its rein.
"Who, by force, prevails over lust and Shaitan?
The battle-ranks of panthers come not from the ant.
"Give me a path, by the holy men of Thy path,
Give me protection from these enemies (lusts).
"O God! by the nature of Thy lordship,

By Thy qualities, matchless and unequaled,

"By—-I await Thy command—-of the pilgrim of the holy house (the Kaaba),

By the buried Mohammed-peace be on him!

"By the extolling of Thee of men, sword-exercising,

Who reckon the man of war, a woman.

"By the worship of old men adorned with devotion,

By the truth of young men, newly risen—

"I pray, saying: In that whirlpool of a breath (death throes),

Help us from the shame of saying, two Gods.

"There is hope from those who perform devotions;

For they make intercession for those devotionless.

"Keep me far from pollution, by the pure;

And hold me excused if any sin passes from me.

"By the old men, back bent with devotion;

Eye from shame of sin stitched to the back of the foot.

"I pray saying: Close not my eye from the face of happiness;

Bind not my tongue at the time of witnessing.

"Hold the lamp of truth opposite my path;

Seep my hand short of doing evil.

"Cause my eyes to turn from that unfit to be seen;

Give me no power, as to disgraceful deeds.

"I am that atom, standing in Thy air,

My existence, on non-existence, through despicability, is one.

"A single ray of the sun of Thy grace is sufficient;

For no one sees me, save in Thy effulgence.

"Glance at the evil one, that he may be better;

A glance from the king is enough for the beggar.

"If Thou, in justice and equity, seizest me, I will complain, saying:

Thy pardon gavest not to me this condition.

"O God! drive me not in contempt from Thy door;
For no other door appears to me.
"And if I become, through ignorance, absent a few days,
Shut not the door in my face when I return.
"What excuse may I bring for the shame of wet-skirtedness,
Unless I offer submission, saying: O independent One!
"I am a poor man; take me not in crime and sin;
The rich man has pity for the poor.
"Why is it necessary to weep for the weakness of my state?
If I am weak, my shelter is Thou.
"O God! in carelessness, we broke the covenant;
What force may the hand of struggle bring against destiny?
"What issues from the hand of our deliberation?
This reliance is, indeed, enough-confession of our sin.
"Whatever I did, Thou didst strike it all together (upset it);
What power may one's self exert against God?
"I take not my head beyond Thy order;
But Thy command thus passes over my head."

A certain one called one of blackish color, ugly;

He gave to him an answer of such a sort that he remained astonished.

"I have not created my own form,
"Which thou consider my fault, saying: I have done ill.
"If I am ugly of face, what business (O sneerer !) hast thou with me?
I am not, in short, the portrayer of the ugly and beautiful."

Beyond that which Thou didst write on my forehead,
Oh Slave-cherisher! I did neither less nor more.
Thou art, in short, the Knower that I am not powerful;
Thou art absolutely powerful—-who am I?
If Thou art my Guide, I arrive at safety;
But if Thou shouldst lose me, I remain behind in journeying.

If the World-Creator affords not assistance,
How may the slave exercise abstinence?
How well said the dervish of short hand,
Who, in the night, vowed; and, in the morning, broke his vow:
"If He gives repentance, it will remain steadfast;
For our covenant is unstable and languid."
By Thy truth! stitch up my eyes from falsehood;
By Thy light! consume me not, to-morrow, in hell.
My face, through poverty, went into the dust;
My sin's dust ascended to Heaven.
Oh, Cloud of Mercy! rain Thou once;
For dust, in the presence of rain, remains not.
Through sin, to me, in this kingdom of the world is no rank;
But to the next world there is no path.
Thou knowest the intention of those tongue-bound;
Thou places the plaster on those heart-wounded.
An idolater was door shut as to his face against the world;
He was loin-girt in an idol's service.
After some years, as to that one of despised religion,
Fate brought before him a difficult matter.
At the idol's foot, in the hope of good,
He helplessly rolled, in the dust of the temple,
Saying: "O idol! I am distressed; help me;
I am ready to die; pity my body."
Many times, in its service, he groaned;
But any deeds for his arrangement issued not.
How may an idol accomplish a person's important affairs,
Which can not drive a fly from its face?
He was confounded, saying: "Oh, one foot-bound in error!
I worshiped thee several years, in folly:
"Accomplish the important matter which I have before me;

Otherwise I will ask it from the Omnipotent."

His face, still stained with dust from (prostration before) the idol,

When the pure God accomplished his wish.

One truths-recognizing became astonished at this;

For his pure time became to him obscured—

Saying: "A mean, false, perturbed worshiper,

His head still with the wine of the wine-tavern intoxicated—

"Washed not his heart from infidelity; nor his religion from treachery—

God fulfilled that desire which he sought!"

His heart descended into this difficulty,

When a message from God came to the ear of his heart,

Saying: "The old man of deficient wisdom, before the idol,

Uttered much; but his prayer was unacceptable.

"If he be also repulsed from Our Court,

Then from the idol to the Lord God—what difference?"

Oh, friend! it is necessary to bind the heart on the Lord God;

Than the idol whatever (or whosoever) it be—who are more helpless?

If thou places thy head in devotion at this door, it is impossible,

That the hand of need should return to thee empty.

O God! we came deficient in work;

We came empty of hand, but hopeful.

I have heard that one intoxicated with the heat of the date wine

Ran to the most sacred place of a masjid.

He bewailed at the threshold of mercy,

Saying: "O Lord! take me to the loftiest Paradise!"

The Mu'azzin seized his collar, saying:

"Make haste, O one careless of wisdom and religion!—-a dog and a masjid.

"What worthy deed didst thou, that thou seeks Paradise?

Grace beseems thee not with an ugly face."

The old man uttered this speech, while the intoxicated one wept,

Saying: "Oh sir! I am drunk; keep thy hand from me.

"Hast thou wonder at the grace of the Omnipotent,

When a simpler is hopeful?

"I say not to thee (oh Mu'azzin!)—-accept my excuse;

The door of repentance is open, and God is helper."

I have constantly shame of the grace of the Merciful One;

For I call my sin great, in comparison with his pardon.

When old age brings down a person from his feet—

When thou seizest not his hand, he rises not from his place.

I am that old man, fallen from his feet;

O God! help me, by Thy own grace.

I say not: Give me greatness and rank;

Pardon me the cause of my wretchedness (sin), and my crime.

If a friend knows a little defect regarding me

He makes me notorious for foolishness.

Thou seeing, and we fearful of each other;

For Thou art the Screen-coverer of sin, and we the screen render.

Men from without the screen have raised a shout on finding a defect;

Thou art always within the screen and screen-coverer.

If slaves, in foolishness, turn their heads from order,

The lords draw the pen (efface the crime).

If Thou pardons sin to the extent of Thy liberality,

There remains no captive in existence.

And if Thou becomes angry to the extent of sin—

Send to hell; and ask not for the balance.

If Thou helps me, I may arrive at the appointed place;

And if Thou casts me down—no one assists.

Who uses violence, if Thou givest assistance?

Who seizes, when thou givest deliverance?

In the place of assembling there will be two parties;

I know not which path they may assign to me.

If my road be from the right hand—it is wonderful;

For only crookedness arose from my hand.

My heart gives, time to time, hope,

That God has shame of my white hair.

I have wonder if He has shame of me,

For shame comes not to me of myself.

Did not Yusuf—who experienced such calamity and imprisonment

When his command became current and his rank lofty—

Pardon the crime of the offspring of Ya'kub?

For a good appearance has virtue.

He imprisoned them not for their bad conduct;

He rejected not their small capital.

We also, from Thy grace, have expectation of this very treatment,

Oh, dear One! forgive the sin of this one, without capital.

No one has seen one of blacker deeds than me

Of whom no deed is approved.

Besides this that to me there is hope of Thy assistance;

To me there is hope of Thy forgiveness.

I have brought no capital, save hope;

O God! make me not hopeless of pardon.

# 7

# THE MASNAVI

*[Horne Introduction]*

*Jalal is famed rather as the chief exponent and teacher of Sufism than as a poet. He became the founder of the sect of "whirling dervishes," or Maulavi [or Mehlavi]. He was born in Afghanistan, the far Eastern Persian land, in 1207, and died in the Turkish domains of Asia Minor, or Rumi, in 1273. His father was a noted Sufi teacher who was driven by persecution to flee from his Afghanistan home, taking his young son with him. Jalal, when only twenty-four, succeeded to his learned father's headship of the great center of learning in Asia Minor, and with youthful enthusiasm spread his impassioned Sufi doctrines far and wide. We are told that in his house there was a central pillar, and that when Jalal was "drowned in the ocean of love," he would take hold of that pillar and set himself turning round it, and improvising his frenzied poetry. When the more conservative Muslims remonstrated with Jalal because his Maulavis danced and sang, even at funerals, Jalal responded "When the human spirit, after years of imprisonment in the cave and dungeon of the body, is at length set free, and wings its flight to the source whence it came, is this not an occasion for rejoicings, thanks, and dancing?" Jalal's religious exposition of Sufism is mainly contained in his "Masnavi", an enormous poetic work in six books, comprising almost 30,000 couplets. The following are selections from that work.*

## THE MUSIC OF LOVE

*Hail to thee, then, O Love, sweet madness!*

*Thou who healest all our infirmities!*

*Who art the Physician of our pride and self-conceit!*
*Who art our Plato and our Galen!*
*Love exalts our earthly bodies to heaven,*
*And makes the very hills to dance with joy!*
*O lover, 'twas Love that gave life to Mount Sinai,*
*When "it quaked, and Moses fell down in a swoon."*
*Did my Beloved only touch me with His lips,*
*I too, like a flute, would burst out into melody.*

## THE BELOVED

*When the rose has faded and the garden is withered,*
*The song of the nightingale is no longer to be heard.*
*The Beloved is all in all, the lover only veils Him;*
*The Beloved is all that lives, the lover a dead thing.*
*When the lover feels no longer love's quickening,*
*He becomes like a bird who has lost its wings. Alas!*
*How can I retain my senses about me,*
*When the Beloved shows not the Light of his countenance?*
*Love is the astrolabe of God's mysteries.*
*A lover may hanker after this love or that love,*
*But at the last he is drawn to the King of Love.*
*However much we describe and explain Love,*
*When we fall in love we are ashamed of our words.*
*Explanation by the tongue makes most things clear,*
*But Love unexplained is better.*
*In one 'twas said, "Leave power and weakness alone;*
*Whatever withdraws thine eyes from God is an idol."*
*In one 'twas said, "Quench not thy earthly torch,*

*That it may be a light to lighten mankind.*

*If thou neglectest regard and care for it,*

*Thou wilt quench at midnight the lamp of Union."*

*Why dost Thou flee from the cries of us on earth?*

*Why pourest Thou sorrow on the heart of the sorrowful?*

*O Thou who, as each new morn dawns from the east,*

*Art seen uprising anew, like a bright fountain!*

*What excuse makest Thou for Thy witcheries?*

*O Thou whose lips are sweeter than sugar,*

*Thou that ever renewest the life of this old world,*

*Hear the cry of this lifeless body and heart!*

*Mustafa became beside himself at that sweet call,*

*His prayer failed on "the night of the early morning halt."*

*He lifted not head from that blissful sleep,*

*So that his morning prayer was put off 'till noon.*

*On that, his wedding night, in the presence of his bride,*

*His pure soul attained to kiss her hands.*

*Love and mistress are both veiled and hidden.*

*Impute it not a fault if I call Him "Bride."*

**HE KNOWS ABOUT IT ALL**

*He who is from head to foot a perfect rose or lily,*

*To him spring brings rejoicing.*

*The useless thorn desires the autumn,*

*That autumn may associate itself with the garden;*

*And hide the rose's beauty and the thorn's shame,*

*That men may not see the bloom of the one and the other's shame;*

*That common stone and pure ruby may appear all as one.*

*True, the Gardener knows the difference in the autumn,*

*But the sight of One is better than the world's sight.*

*Whoso recognizes and confesses his own defects*

*Is hastening in the way that leads to Perfection!*

*But he advances not toward the Almighty*

*Who fancies himself to be perfect.*

*Whatsoever is perceived by sense He annuls,*

*But He stablishes that which is hidden from the senses.*

*The lover's love is visible, his Beloved hidden.*

*The Friend is absent, the distraction He causes present.*

*Renounce these affections for outward forms,*

*Love depends not on outward form or face.*

*Whatever is beloved is not a mere empty form,*

*Whether your beloved be of earth or heaven.*

*Whatever is the form you have fallen in love with—*

*Why do you forsake it the moment life leaves it?*

*The form is still there; whence then this disgust at it?*

*Ah! lover, consider well what is really your beloved.*

*If a thing perceived by outward senses is the beloved,*

*Then all who retain senses must still love it;*

*And since Love increases constancy,*

*How can constancy fail while form abides?*
*But the truth is, the sun's beams strike the wall,*
*And the wall only reflects that borrowed light.*
*Why give your heart to mere stones, O simpleton?*
*Go! Seek the Source of Light which shineth alway!*

**THE RELIGION OF LOVE**

*The sect of lovers is distinct from all others,*
*Lovers have a religion and a faith of their own.*
*Though the ruby has no stamp, what matters it?*
*Love is fearless in the midst of the sea of fear.*
*Pain is a treasure, for it contains mercies;*
*The kernel is soft when the rind is scraped off.*
*O brother, the place of darkness and cold*
*Is the fountain of Life and the cup of ecstasy.*
*So also is endurance of pain and sickness and disease.*
*For from abasement proceeds exaltation.*
*The spring seasons are hidden in the autumns,*
*And the autumns are charged with springs.*
*If spiritual manifestations had been sufficient,*
*The creation of the world had been needless and vain.*
*If spiritual thought were equivalent to love of God,*
*Outward forms of temples and prayers would not exist.*
*"We bow our heads before His edict and ordinance,*
*We stake precious life to gain His favor.*
*While the thought of the Beloved fills our hearts,*

*All our work is to do Him service and spend life for Him.*
*Wherever He kindles His destructive torch,*
*Myriads of lovers' souls are burnt therewith.*
*The lovers who dwell within the sanctuary*
*Are moths burnt with the torch of the Beloved's face.*
*"O heart, haste thither, for God will shine upon you,*
*And seem to you a sweet garden instead of a terror.*
*He will infuse into your soul a new Soul,*
*So as to fill you, like a goblet, with wine.*
*Take up your abode in His Soul!*
*Take up your abode in heaven, O bright full moon!*
*Like the heavenly Scribe, He will open your heart's book*
*That He may reveal mysteries unto you.*
*The sea itself is one thing, the foam another;*
*Neglect the foam, and regard the sea with your eyes.*
*Waves of foam rise from the sea night and day.*
*You look at the foam ripples and not at the mighty sea.*
*We, like boats, are tossed hither and thither,*
*We are blind though we are on the bright ocean.*
*Ah! you who are asleep in the boat of the body,*
*You see the water; behold the Water of waters!*
*Under the water you see there is another Water moving it.*
*Within the spirit is a Spirit that calls it.*
*When you have accepted the Light, O beloved,*
*When you behold what is veiled without a veil,*
*Like a star you will walk upon the heavens.*

## WHERE LOVE IS

*A damsel said to her lover, "O fond youth,*
*You have visited many cities in your travels;*
*Which of those cities seems most delightful to you?"*
*He made answer, "The city wherein my love dwells,*
*In whatever nook my queen alights;*
*Though it be as the eye of a needle, 'tis a wide plain;*
*Wherever her Yusuf-like face shines as a moon,*
*Though it be the bottom of a well, 'tis Paradise.*
*With thee, my love, hell itself were heaven.*
*With thee a prison would be a rose-garden.*
*With thee hell would be a mansion of delight,*
*Without thee lilies and roses would be as flames of fire!"*
*No lover ever seeks union with his beloved,*
*But his beloved is also seeking union with him.*
*But the lover's love makes his body lean,*
*While the Beloved's love makes her fair and lusty.*
*When in this heart the lightning spark of love arises,*
*Be sure this Love is reciprocated in that heart.*
*When the Love of God arises in thy heart,*
*Without doubt God also feels love for thee.*
*The Love of the soul is for Life and the Living One,*
*Because its origin is the Soul not bound to place.*
*The Love of the soul is for wisdom and knowledge,*
*That of the body for houses, gardens, and vineyards;*
*The love of the soul is for things exalted on high,*
*That of the body for acquisition of goods and food.*

*The Love, too, of Him on high is directed to the soul:*
*Know this, for "Be loves them that love Him."*
*The sum is this: that whoso seeks another,*
*The soul of that other who is sought inclines to him.*
*O Israfil of the resurrection-day of Love!*
*O Love, Love, and heart's desire of Love!*
*Let thy first boon to me be this:*
*To lend thine ear to my orisons,*
*Though thou knowest my condition clearly,*
*O protector of slaves, listen to my speech.*
*A thousand times, O prince incomparable,*
*Has my reason taken flight in desire to see thee,*
*And to hear thee and to listen to thy words,*
*And to behold thy life-giving smiles.*
*Thy inclining thine ear to my supplications*
*Is as a caress to my misguided soul.*

## DESTROY NOT EARTHLY BEAUTY

*Tear not thy plumage off, it can not be replaced;*
*Disfigure not thy face in wantonness, O fair one!*
*That face which is bright as the forenoon sun—*
*To disfigure it were a grievous sin.*
*'Twere paganism to mar such a face as thine!*
*The moon itself would weep to lose sight of it!*
*Knowest thou not the beauty of thine own face?*
*Quit this temper that leads thee to war with thyself!*
*It is the claws of thine own foolish thoughts*
*That in spite wound the face of thy quiet soul.*
*Know such thoughts to be claws fraught with poison.*

*Which score deep wounds on the face of thy soul.*
*Thus spake cursed Iblis to the Almighty,*
*"I want a mighty trap to catch human game withal!"*
*God gave him gold and silver and troops and horses,*
*Saying, "You can catch my creatures with these."*
*Iblis said, "Bravo!" but at the same time hung his lip,*
*And frowned sourly like a bitter orange.*
*Then God offered gold and jewels from precious mines*
*To that laggard in the faith,*
*Saying, "Take these other traps, O cursed one."*
*But Iblis said, "Give me more, O blessed Defender."*
*God gave him succulent and sweet and costly wines,*
*And also store of silken garments.*
*But Iblis said, "O Lord, I want more aids than these,*
*In order to bind men in my twisted rope*
*So firmly that Thy adorers, who are valiant men,*
*May not, man-like, break my bonds asunder."*
*When at last God showed him the beauty of women,*
*Which bereaves men of reason and self-control,*
*Then Iblis clapped his hands and began to dance,*
*Saying, "Give me these; I shall quickly prevail with these!"*
*Lovers and beloved have both perished;*
*And not themselves only, but their love as well.*
*'Tis God alone who agitates these nonentities,*
*Making one nonentity fall in love with another.*
*In the heart that is no heart envy comes to a head,*
*Thus Being troubles nonentity.*

## ALLAH'S CALL

*"O angels, bring him back to me.*

*Since the eyes of his heart were set on Hope,*

*Without care for consequence I set him free,*

*And draw the pen through the record of his sins!"*

A lover was once admitted to the presence of his mistress, but, instead of embracing her, he pulled out a paper of sonnets and read them to her, describing her perfections and charms and his own love toward her at length. His mistress said to him, "You are now in my presence, and these lovers' sighs and invocations are a waste of time.

It is not the part of a true lover to waste his time in this way. It shows that I am not the real object of your affection, but that what you really love is your own effusions and ecstatic raptures. I see, as it were, the water which I have longed for before me, and yet you withhold it. I am, as it were, in Bulghara, and the object of your love is in Cathay. One who is really loved is the single object of her lover, the Alpha and Omega of his desires. As for you, you are wrapped up in your own amorous raptures, depending on the varying states of your own feelings, instead of being wrapped up in me."

Eternal Life is gained by utter abandonment of one's own life. When God appears to His ardent lover the lover is absorbed in Him, and not so much as a hair of the lover remains. True lovers are as shadows, and when the sun shines in glory the shadows vanish away. He is a true lover to God to whom God says, "I am thine, and thou art Mine!"

## LOVE NEEDS NO MEDIATOR

When one has attained Union with God he has no need of intermediaries. Prophets and apostles are needled as links to connect ordinary man with God, but he who hears the "inner voice" within him has no need to listen to outward words, even of apostles. Although that intercession is himself dwelling in God, yet my state is higher and more lovely than his. Though he is God's agent, yet I desire not his intercession to save me from evil sent me by God, for evil at God's hand seems to me good. What seems mercy and kindness to the vulgar seems wrath and vengeance to God-intoxicated saints.

## HUMANITY THE REFLECTION OF THE BELOVED

Parrots are taught to speak without understanding the words. The method is to place a mirror between the parrot and the trainer. The trainer, hidden by the mirror, utters the words, and the parrot, seeing his own reflection in the mirror, fancies another parrot is speaking, and imitates all that is said by the trainer behind the mirror. So God uses prophets and saints as mirrors whereby to instruct men, *viz.*, the bodies of these saints and prophets; and men, when they hear the words proceeding from these mirrors, are utterly ignorant that they are really being spoken by "Universal Reason" or the "Word of God" behind the mirror of the saints.

Earthly forms are only shadows of the Sun of Truth—a cradle for babes, but too small to hold those who have grown to spiritual manhood.

## THE VISION OF ETERNAL TRUTH

The end and object of all negation is to attain to subsequent affirmation, as the negation in the creed, "There is no God," finds its complement and purpose in the affirmation "but God." Just so the purpose of negation of self is to clear the way for the apprehension of the fact that there is no existence but the One. The intoxication of Life and its pleasures and occupations veils the Truth from men's eyes, and they ought to pass on to the spiritual intoxication which makes men beside themselves and lifts them to the beatific vision of eternal Truth.

## THE WINE EVERLASTING

*O babbler, while thy soul is drunk with mere date wine,*

*Thy spirit hath not tasted the genuine grapes.*

*For the token of thy having seen that divine Light*

*Is this, to withdraw thyself from the house of pride.*

*When those Egyptian women sacrificed their reason,*

*They penetrated the mansion of Joseph's love;*

*The Cupbearer of Life bore away their reason*

*They were filled with wisdom of the world without end.*

*Joseph's beauty was only an offshoot of God's beauty:*

*Be lost, then, in God's beauty more than those women.*

*What ear has told you falsely eye will tell truly.*

*Then ear, too, will acquire the properties of an eye;*

*Your ears, now worthless as wool, will become gems;*

*Yea, your whole body will become a mirror,*

*It will be as an eye of a bright gem in your bosom.*

*First the hearing of the ear enables you to form ideas,*

*Then these ideas guide you to the Beloved.*

*Strive, then, to increase the number of these ideas,*

*That they may guide you, like Majnun, to the Beloved.*

*Yea, O sleeping heart, know the kingdom that endures not*

*Forever and ever is only a mere dream.*

*I marvel how long you will indulge in vain illusion,*

*Which has seized you by the throat like a headsman.*

*Know that even in this world there is a place of refuge;*

*Harken not to the unbeliever who denies it.*

*His argument is this: he says again and again,*

*"If there were aught beyond this life we should see it."*

*But if the child see not the state of reason,*

*Does the man of reason therefore forsake reason?*
*And if the man of reason sees not the state of Love,*
*Is the blessed moon of Love thereby eclipsed?*

### THE LOVER'S CRY TO THE BELOVED

*"My back is broken by the conflict of my thoughts;*
*O Beloved One, come and stroke my head in mercy!*
*The palm of Thy hand on my head gives me rest,*
*Thy hand is a sign of Thy bounteous providence.*
*Remove not Thy shadow from my head,*
*I am afflicted, afflicted, afflicted!*
*Sleep has deserted my eyes*
*Through my longing for Thee, O Envy of cypresses!*
*O take my life, Thou art the Source of Life!*
*For apart from Thee I am wearied of my life.*
*I am a lover well versed in lovers' madness,*
*I am weary of learning and sense."*

### SORROW TURNED TO JOY

*"He who extracts the rose from the thorn*
*Can also turn this winter into spring.*
*He who exalts the heads of the cypresses*
*Is able also out of sadness to bring joy."*

### THE GIFTS OF THE BELOVED

*Where will you find one more liberal than God?*
*He buys the worthless rubbish which is your wealth,*
*He pays you the Light that illumines your heart.*
*He accepts these frozen and lifeless bodies of yours,*
*And gives you a Kingdom beyond what you dream of,*

*He takes a few drops of your tears,*
*And gives you the Divine Fount sweeter than sugar.*
*He takes your sighs fraught with grief and sadness,*
*And for each sigh gives rank in heaven as interest.*
*In return for the sigh-wind that raised tear-clouds,*
*God gave Abraham the title of "Father of the Faithful."*
*Thou art hidden from us, though the heavens are filled*
*With Thy Light, which is brighter than sun and moon!*
*Thou art hidden, yet revealest our hidden secrets!*
*Thou art the Source that causes our rivers to flow.*
*Thou art hidden in Thy essence, but seen by Thy bounties.*
*Thou art like the water, and we like the millstone.*
*Thou art like the wind, and we like the dust;*
*The wind is unseen, but the dust is seen by all.*
*Thou art the Spring, and we the sweet green garden;*
*Spring is not seen, though its gifts are seen.*
*Thou art as the Soul, we as hand and foot;*
*Soul instructs hand and foot to hold and take.*
*Thou art as Reason, we like the tongue;*
*'Tis reason that teaches the tongue to speak.*
*Thou art as Joy, and we are laughing;*
*The laughter is the consequence of the joy.*
*Our every motion every moment testifies,*
*For it proves the presence of the Everlasting God.*

## EXERT YOURSELVES

*"Trust in God, yet tie the camel's leg.'*
*Hear the adage, 'The worker is the friend of God';*
*Through trust in Providence neglect not to use means.*
*Go, O Fatalists, practise trust with self-exertion,*
*Exert yourself to attain your objects, bit by bit.*
*In order to succeed, strive and exert yourselves;*
*If you strive not for your objects, ye are fools."*

## THE WISDOM OF THE WEAK

*"O friends, God has given me inspiration.*
*Oftentimes strong counsel is suggested to the weak.*
*The wit taught by God to the bee*
*Is withheld from the lion and the wild ass.*
*It fills its cells with liquid sweets,*
*For God opens the door of this knowledge to it.*
*The skill taught by God to the silkworm*
*Is a learning beyond the reach of the elephant.*
*The earthly Adam was taught of God names,*
*So that his glory reached the seventh heaven.*
*He laid low the name and fame of the angels,*
*Yet blind indeed are they whom God dooms to doubt!"*

## WHITE NIGHTS

*Every night Thou freest our spirits from the body*
*And its snare, making them pure as rased tablets.*
*Every night spirits are released from this cage,*
*And set free, neither lording it nor lorded over.*
*At night prisoners are unaware of their prison,*
*At night kings are unaware of their majesty.*

## THE KINGLY SOUL

*The kingly soul lays waste the body,*
*And after its destruction he builds it anew.*
*Happy the soul who for love of God*
*Has lavished family, wealth, and goods!—*
*Has destroyed its house to find the Hidden Treasure,*
*And with that Treasure has rebuilt it in fairer sort;*
*Has dammed up the stream and cleansed the channel,*
*And then turned a fresh stream into the channel.*

## SAINT AND HYPOCRITE

*Watch the face of each one, regard it well,*
*It may be by serving thou wilt recognize Truth's face.*
*As there are many demons with men's faces,*
*It is wrong to join hand with every one.*
*When the fowler sounds his decoy whistle,*
*That the birds may be beguiled by that snare,*
*The birds hear that call simulating a bird's call,*
*And, descending from the air, find net and knife.*
*So vile hypocrites steal the language of Dervishes,*
*In order to beguile the simple with their trickery.*
*The works of the righteous are light and heat,*
*The works of the evil treachery and shamelessness.*
*They make stuffed lions to scare the simple,*
*They give the title of Mohammed to false Musailima.*
*But Musailima retained the name of "Liar,"*
*And Mohammed that of "Sublimest of beings."*

*That wine of God (the righteous) yields a perfume of musk;*
*Other wine (the evil) is reserved for penalties and pains.*

## HARSHNESS AND ADORATION

*Let me then, I say, make complaint*
*Of the severity of that Fickle Fair One.*
*I cry, and my cries sound sweet in His ear;*
*He requires from the two worlds cries and groans.*
*How shall I not wail under His chastening hand?*
*How shall I not be in the number of those bewitched by Him?*
*How shall I be other than night without His day?*
*Without the vision of His face that illumes the day?*
*His bitters are very sweets to my soul,*
*I am enamored of my own grief and pain,*
*For it makes me well-pleasing to my peerless King.*
*I use the dust of my grief as salve for my eyes,*
*That my eyes, like seas, may team with pearls.*

## THE DIVINE ABSORPTION

*Do me justice, O Thou who art the glory of the just,*
*Who art the throne, and I the lintel of Thy door!*
*But, in sober truth, where are throne and doorway?*
*Where are "We" and "I"? There where our Beloved is!*
*O Thou, who art exempt from "Us" and "Me,"*
*Who pervadest the spirits of all men and women;*
*When man and woman become one, Thou art that One!*

*When their union is dissolved, lo! Thou abidest!*

*Thou hast made these "Us" and "Me" for this purpose,*

*To wit, to play chess with them by Thyself.*

*When Thou shalt become one entity with "Us" and "You,"*

*Then wilt Thou show true affection for these lovers.*

*When these "We" and "Ye" shall all become One Soul,*

*Then they will be lost and absorbed in the "Beloved."*

## LOVE MORE THAN SORROW AND JOY

*Come then, O Lord!*

*Who are exalted above description and explanation!*

*Is it possible for the bodily eye to behold Thee?*

*Can mind of man conceive Thy frowns and Thy smiles?*

*Are hearts, when bewitched by Thy smiles and frowns,*

*In a fit state to see the vision of Thyself?*

*When our hearts are bewitched by Thy smiles and frowns,*

*Can we gain Life from these two alternating states?*

*The fertile garden of Love, as it is boundless,*

*Contains other fruits besides joy and sorrow.*

*The true lover is exalted above these two states,*

*He is fresh and green independently of autumn or spring!*

*Pay tithe on Thy beauty, O Beauteous One!*

*Tell forth the tale of the Beloved, every whit!*

*The heart of the harper was emancipated.*

*Like a soul he was freed from weeping and rejoicing,*
*His old life died, and he was regenerated.*
*Amazement fell upon him at that moment,*
*For he was exalted above earth and heaven,*
*An uplifting of the heart surpassing all uplifting.*
*I can not describe it; if you can, say on!*
*Ecstasy and words beyond all ecstatic words—*
*Immersion in the glory of the Lord of glory!*
*Immersion wherefrom was no extrication—*
*As it were identification with the Very Ocean!*
*When night returns and 'tis the time of the sky's levee,*
*The stars that were hidden come forth to their work.*
*The people of the world lie unconscious,*
*With veils drawn over their faces, and asleep;*
*But when the morn shall burst forth and the sun arise*
*Every creature will raise its head from its couch;*
*To the unconscious God will restore consciousness;*
*They will stand in rings as slaves with rings in ears;*
*Dancing and clapping hands with songs of praise,*
*Singing with joy, "Our Lord hath restored us to life!"*

## SEPARATION

*Nothing is bitterer than severance from Thee,*
*Without Thy shelter there is naught but perplexity.*
*Our worldly goods rob us of our heavenly goods,*
*Our body rends the garment of our soul.*
*Our hands, as it were, prey on our feet;*
*Without reliance on Thee how can we live?*

## GOD'S LIGHT

*'Tis God's Light that illumines the senses' light,*
*That is the meaning of "Light upon light."*
*The senses' light draws us earthward.*
*God's Light calls us heavenward.*
*When love of God kindles a flame in the inward man,*
*He burns, and is freed from effects.*
*He has no need of signs to assure him of Love,*
*For Love casts its own Light up to heaven.*

## THE BELIEVER'S HEART

*The Prophet said that God has declared,*
*"I am not contained in aught above or below,*
*I am not contained in earth or sky, or even*
*In highest heaven. Know this for a surety, O beloved!*
*Yet am I contained in the believer's heart!*
*If ye seek Me, search in such hearts!"*

## SELF-SATISFACTION

*No sickness worse than fancying thyself perfect*
*Can infect thy soul, O arrogant, misguided one!*
*Shed many tears of blood from eyes and heart,*
*That this self-satisfaction may be driven out.*
*The fate of Iblis lay in saying, "I am better than He,"*
*And this same weakness lurks in the souls of all creatures.*

## TRUE KNOWLEDGE

*The knowledge which is not of Him is a burden;*
*Knowledge which comes not immediately from Him*

*Endures no longer than the rouge of the tire-woman.*

*Nevertheless, if you bear this burden in a right spirit*

*'Twill be removed, and you will obtain joy.*

*See you bear not that burden out of vainglory,*

*Then you will behold a store of True Knowledge within.*

*When you mount the steed of this True Knowledge,*

*Straightway the burden will fall from your back.*

## THE FLAME OF LOVE

*How long wilt thou dwell on words and empty shows?*

*A burning heart is what I want; consort with burning!*

*Kindle in thy heart the flame of Love,*

*And burn up utterly thoughts and fine expressions.*

*O Moses! the lovers of fair rites are one class,*

*They whose hearts and souls burn with Love, another.*

A woman bore many children in succession, but none of them lived beyond the age of three or four months. In great distress she cried to God, and then beheld in a vision the beautiful gardens of Paradise, and many fair mansions therein, and upon one of these mansions she read her own name inscribed. And a voice from heaven informed her that God would accept the sorrows she had endured in lieu of her blood shed in holy war, as, owing to her sex, she was unable to go out to battle like the men. On looking again, the woman beheld in Paradise all the children she had lost, and she cried, "O Lord! they were lost to me, but safe with Thee!"

## THE OPTIMISTIC ROSE

*In this tale there is a warning for thee, O Soul,*

*That thou mayest acquiesce in God's ordinances,*

*And be wary and not doubt God's benevolence,*
*When sudden misfortune befalls thee.*
*Let others grow pale from fear of ill fortune,*
*Do thou smile like the rose at loss and gain;*
*For the rose, though its petals be torn asunder,*
*Still smiles on, and it is never cast down.*

## THE TRUE MOSQUE

*Fools laud and magnify the mosque,*
*While they strive to oppress holy men of heart.*
*But the former is mere form, the latter spirit and truth.*
*The only true mosque is that in the hearts of saints.*
*The mosque that is built in the hearts of the saints*
*Is the place of worship of all, for God dwells there.*
*So long as the hearts of the saints are not afflicted,*
*God never destroys the nation.*

## IGNORANCE

*Blood is impure, yet its stain is removed by water;*
*But that impurity of ignorance is more lasting,*
*Seeing that without the blessed water of God*
*It is not banished from the man who is subject to it.*
*O that thou wouldst turn thy face to thy own prayers,*

And say, "Ah! my prayers are as defective as my being; O requite me good for evil!"

*"Pray in this wise and allay your difficulties:*
*'Give us good in the house of our present world,*
*And give us good in the house of our next world.*

*Make our path pleasant as a garden,*
*And be Thou, O Holy One, our goal!'"*

## ALL RELIGIONS ARE ONE

*In the adorations and benedictions of righteous men*
*The praises of all the prophets are kneaded together.*
*All their praises are mingled into one stream,*
*All the vessels are emptied into one ewer.*
*Because He that is praised is, in fact, only One.*
*In this respect all religions are only one religion.*
*Because all praises are directed toward God's Light,*
*These various forms and figures are borrowed from it.*

8

## The Fairest Land

*"Tell me, gentle traveler, thou*
*Who hast wandered far and wide,*
*Seen the sweetest roses blow,*
*And the brightest rivers glide;*
*Say, of all thine eyes have seen,*
*Which the fairest land has been?*
*"Lady, shall I tell thee where*
*Nature seems most blest and fair,*
*Far above all climes beside?—*
*'Tis where those we love abide:*
*And that little spot is best*
*Which the loved one's foot hath pressed.*
*"Though it be a fairy space,*
*Wide and spreading is the place;*
*Though 'twere but a barren mound,*
*'Twould become enchanted ground.*
*"With thee yon sandy waste would seem*
*The margin of Al Cawthar's stream;*
*And thou canst make a dungeon's gloom*
*A bower where new-born roses bloom."*

## POEMS FROM THE *DIVAN-I SHAMS-I TABRIZ*

### *I*

*The man of God is drunken without wine,*
*The man of God is full without meat.*
*The man of God is distraught and bewildered,*
*The man of God has no food or sleep.*
*The man of God is a king "neath dervish-cloak,*
*The man of God is a treasure in a ruin.*
*The man of God is not of air and earth,*
*The man of God is not of fire and water.*
*The man of God is a boundless sea,*
*The man of God rains pearls without a cloud.*
*The man of God has hundred moons and skies,*
*The man of God has hundred suns.*
*The man of God is made wise by the Truth,*
*The man of God is not learned from book.*
*The man of God is beyond infidelity and religion,*
*To the man of God right and wrong are alike.*
*The man of God has ridden away from Not-being,*
*The man of God is gloriously attended.*
*The man of God is concealed, Shamsi Din;*
*The man of God do you seek and find!*

### *II*

*What is to be done, O Moslems? for I do not recognize myself.*

*I am neither Christian, nor Jew, nor Gabr [Magian], nor Moslem.*

*I am not of the East, nor of the West, nor of the land, nor of the sea;*

*I am not of Nature's mint, nor of the circling heavens.*

*I am not of earth, nor of water, nor of air, nor of fire;*

*I am not of the empyrean, nor of the dust, nor of existence, nor of entity.*

*I am not of India, nor of China, nor of Bulghar, nor of Saqsin;*

*I am not of the kingdom of 'Iraqain, nor of the country of Khurasan.*

*I am not of this world, nor of the next, nor of Paradise, nor of Hell;*

*I am not of Adam, nor of Eve, nor of Eden and Rizwan.*

*My place is the Placeless, my trace is the Traceless;*

*'Tis neither body nor soul, for I belong to the soul of the Beloved.*

*I have put duality away, I have seen that the two worlds are one;*

*One I seek, One I know, One I see, One I call.*

He is the first, He is the lest, He is the outward, He is the inward;

*I know none other except "Ya Hu" [Yahweh] and "Ya man Hu" ["O He who is"].*

*I am intoxicated with Love's cup, the two worlds have passed out of my ken;*

*I have no business save carouse and revelry.*

*If once in my life I spent a moment without you,*

*From that time and from that hour I repent of my life.*

*If once in this world I win a moment with you,*

*I will trample on both worlds, I will dance in triumph for ever.*

*O Shamsi Tabriz, I am so drunken in this world,*

*That except of drunkenness and revelry I have no tale to tell.*

*III*

*No joy have I found in the two worlds apart from you, Beloved.*

*Many wonders I have seen: I have not seen a wonder like you.*

*They say that blazing fire is the infidel's portion:*

*I have seen none, save Abu Lahab, excluded from your fire.*

*Often have I laid the spiritual ear at the window of the heart:*

*I heard much discourse, but the lips I did not see.*

*Of a sudden you did lavish grace upon your servant:*

*I saw no cause for it but your infinite kindness.*

*O chosen Cup-bearer, O apple of mine eyes, the like of you*

*Ne'er appeared in Persia, nor in Arabia have I found it.*

*Pour out wine 'till I become a wanderer from myself;*

*For in selfhood and existence I have felt only fatigue.*

*O you who are milk and sugar, O you who are sun and moon,*

*O you who are mother and father, I have known no kin but you.*

*O indestructible Love, O divine Minstrel,*

*You are both stay and refuge: a name equal to you I have not found.*

*We are pieces of steel, and your love is the magnet:*

*You are the source of all aspiration, in myself I have seen none.*

*Silence, O brother! put learning and culture away:*

*'Till you named culture, I knew no culture but you.*

*IV*

*Grasp the skirt of his favor, for on a sudden he will flee;*

*But draw him not, as an arrow, for he will flee from the bow.*

*What delusive forms does he take, what tricks does he invent!*

*If he is present in form, he will flee by the way of spirit.*

*Seek him in the sky, he shines in water, like the moon;*

*When you come into the water, he will flee to the sky.*

*Seek him in the placeless, he will sign you to place;*

*When you seek him in place, he will flee to the placeless.*

*As the arrow speeds from the bow, like the bird of your imagination,*

*Know that the Absolute will certainly flee from the Imaginary.*

*I will flee from this and that, not for weariness, but for fear*

*That my gracious Beauty will flee from this and that.*

*As the wind I am fleet of foot, from love of the rose I am like the zephyr;*

*The rose in dread of autumn will flee from the garden.*

*His name will flee, when it sees an attempt at speech,*

*So that you cannot even say, "Such an one will flee."*

*He will flee from you, so that if you limn his picture,*

*The picture will fly from the tablet, the impression will flee from the soul.*

***V***

*A beauty that all night long teaches love-tricks to Venus and the moon,*

*Whose two eyes by their witchery seal up the two eyes of heaven.*

*Look to your hearts! I, whate'er betide, O Moslems,*

*Am so mingled with him that no heart is mingled with me.*

*I was born of his love at the first, I gave him my heart at the last;*

*When the fruit springs from the bough, on that bough it hangs.*

*The tip of his curl is saying, "Ho! betake you to rope-dancing."*

*The cheek of his candle is saying, "Where is a moth that it may burn?"*

*For the sake of dancing on that rope, O heart, make haste, become a hoop;*

*Cast yourself on the flame, when his candle is lit.*

*You will never more endure without the flame, when you have known the rapture of burning;*

*If the water of life should come to you, it would not stir you from the flame.*

***VI***

*David said: "O Lord, since you have no need of us,*

*Say, then, what wisdom was there in creating the two worlds?"*

*God said to him: "O temporal man, I was a hidden treasure;*

*I sought that that treasure of loving kindness and bounty should be revealed.*

*I displayed a mirror—its face the heart, its back the world—*

*Its back is better than its face—if the face is unknown to you."*

*When straw is mixed with clay, how should the mirror be successful?*

*When you part the straw from the clay, the mirror becomes clear.*

*Grape-juice does not turn to wine, unless it ferment awhile in the jar;*

*Would you have your heart grow bright, you must take a little trouble.*

*The soul which issued forth from the body—my king said to it:*

*"You are come even as you went: where are the traces of my benefactions?"*

*'Tis notorious that copper by alchemy becomes gold:*

*Our copper has been transmuted by this rare alchemy.*

*From God's grace this sun wants no crown or robe:*

*He is cap to a hundred bald men and cloak to ten naked.*

*Child, Jesus sate on an ass for humility's sake:*

*How else should the zephyr ride on the back of an ass?*

*O spirit, make your head in search and seeking like the water of a stream,*

*And O reason, to gain eternal life tread everlastingly the way of death.*

*Keep God in remembrance 'till self is forgotten,*

*That you may be lost in the Called, without distraction of caller and call.*

*VII*

*You I choose, of all the world, alone;*

*Will you suffer me to sit in grief?*

*My heart is as a pen in your hand,*

*You are the cause if I am glad or melancholy.*

*Save what you will, what will have I?*

*Save what you show, what do I see?*

*You make grow out of me now a thorn and now a rose;*

*Now I smell roses and now pull thorns.*

*If you keep me that, that I am;*

*If you would have me this, I am this.*

*In the vessel where you give color to the soul*

*Who am I, what is my love and hate?*

*You were first, and last you shall be;*

*Make my last better than my first.*

*When you are hidden, I am of the infidels;*

*When you are manifest, I am of the faithful.*

*I have nothing, except you have bestowed it;*

*What do you seek from my bosom and sleeve?*

*VIII*

*When my bier moves on the day of death,*

*Think not my heart is in this world.*

*Do not weep for me and cry "Woe, woe!"*

*You will fall in the devil's snare: that is woe.*

*When you see my hearse, cry not "Parted, parted!"*

*Union and meeting are mine in that hour.*

*If you commit me to the grave, say not "Farewell, farewell!"*

*For the grave is a curtain hiding the communion of Paradise.*

*After beholding descent, consider resurrection;*

*Why should setting be injurious to the sun and moon?*

*To you it seems a setting, but 'tis a rising;*

*Tho' the vault seems a prison, 'tis the release of the soul.*

*What seed went down into the earth but it grew?*

*Why this doubt of yours as regards the seed of man?*

*What bucket was lowered but it came out brimful?*

*Why should the Joseph of the spirit complain of the well?*

*Shut your mouth on this side and open it beyond,*

*For in placeless air will be your triumphal song.*

## VERSES IN PRAISE OF GOD, C. 1370 CE

### [Horne Introduction]

*The name "Hafiz" means "strong-memoried," and was given as a phrase of honor to the poet when, as a young boy, he recited the entire Qur'an by heart. He was born at Shiraz, in southern Persia, in 1325, and died there in 1389. Hafiz was one of the world's greatest masters of lyric verse. Both he and Jami are Sufis, but in a very different mood. The Sufism of Hafiz is like that of Umar Khayyam, i.e., Hafiz confines himself so wholly to the praise of wine and love, that questions arose whether he was always thinking about the joys of the spirit.*

## IN PRAISE OF HIS OWN VERSES

*The beauty of these verses baffles praise:*
*What guide is needed to the solar blaze?*
*Extol that artist by whose pencil's aid*
*The virgin, Thought, so richly is arrayed.*
*For her no substitute can reason show,*
*Nor any like her human judgment know.*
*This verse, a miracle, or magic white—*
*Brought down some voice from Heaven, or Gabriel bright?*
*By me as by none else are secrets sung,*
*No pearls of poesy like mine are strung*

## A PERSIAN SONG

*Sweet maid, if thou wouldst charm my sight,*
*And bid these arms thy neck enfold;*
*That rosy cheek, that lily hand,*
*Would give thy poet more delight*
*Than all Bocara's vaunted gold,*
*Than all the gems of Samarkand.*
*Boy, let yon liquid ruby flow,*
*And bid thy pensive heart be glad,*
*Whate'er the frowning zealots say:*
*Tell them, their Eden can not show*
*A stream so clear as Rocnabad,*
*A bow'r so sweet as Mosellay.*
*Oh! when these fair perfidious maids,*
*Whose eyes our secret haunts infest,*
*Their dear destructive charms display,*

*Each glance my tender heart invades,*
*And robs my wounded soul of rest,*
*As Tartars seize their destined prey.*
*In vain with love our bosoms glow:*
*Can all our tears, can all our sighs,*
*New luster to those charms impart?*
*Can cheeks, where living roses blow,*
*Where Nature spreads her richest dyes,*
*Require the borrowed gloss of art?*
*Speak not of fate:—ah! change the theme,*
*And talk of odors, talk of wine,*
*Talk of the flow'rs that round us bloom:*
*'Tis all a cloud, 'tis all a dream;*
*To love and joy thy thoughts confine,*
*Nor hope to pierce the sacred gloom.*
*Beauty has such resistless pow'r,*
*That ev'n the chaste Egyptian dame*
*Sighed for the blooming Hebrew boy:*
*For her how fatal was the hour*
*When to the banks of Nilus came*
*A youth so lovely and so coy!*
*But ah! sweet maid, my counsel hear*
*(Youth should attend when those advise*
*Whom long experience renders sage)*
*While music charms the ravished ear,*
*While sparkling cups delight our eyes,*
*Be gay, and scorn the frowns of age.*
*What cruel answer have I heard?*

*And yet, by Heav'n, I love thee still:*
*Can aught be cruel from thy lips?*
*Yet say, how fell that bitter word*
*From lips which streams of sweetness fill,*
*Which naught but drops of honey sip?*
*Go boldly forth, my simple lay,*
*Whose accents flow with artless ease,*
*Like Orient pearls at random strung;*
*Thy notes are sweet, the damsels say,*
*But oh! far sweeter, if they please*
*The Nymph for whom these notes are sung.*

## THE FEAST OF SPRING

*My breast is filled with roses,*
*My cup is crowned with wine,*
*And by my side reposes*
*The maid I hail as mine.*
*The monarch, wheresoe'er he be,*
*Is but a slave compared to me!*
*Their glare no torches throwing*
*Shall in our bower be found;*
*Her eyes, like moonbeams glowing,*
*Cast light enough around:*
*And well all odors I can spare,*
*Who scent the perfume of her hair.*
*The honey-dew thy charm might borrow,*
*Thy lip alone to me is sweet;*
*When thou art absent, faint with sorrow*
*I hide me in some lone retreat.*

*Why talk to me of power or fame?—*
*What are those idle toys to me?*
*Why ask the praises of my name?*
*My joy, my triumph is in thee!*
*How blest am I! around me, swelling,*
*The notes of melody arise;*
*I hold the cup, with juice excelling,*
*And gaze upon thy radiant eyes.*
*O Hafiz!—never waste thy hours*
*Without the cup, the lute, and love!*
*For 'tis the sweetest time of flowers,*
*And none these moments shall reprove.*
*The nightingales around thee sing,*
*It is the joyous feast of spring.*

## MYSTIC ODE

*In wide Eternity's vast space,*
*Where no beginning was, wert Thou:*
*The rays of all-pervading grace*
*Beneath Thy veil flamed on Thy brow.*
*Then Love and Nature sprang to birth,*
*And Life and Beauty filled the earth.*
*Awake, my soul! pour forth thy praise,*
*To that great Being anthems raise—*
*That wondrous Architect who said,*
*"Be formed," and this great orb was made.*
*Since first I heard the blissful sound—*
*"To man My Spirit's breath is given";*
*I knew, with thankfulness profound,*

*His sons we are—our Home is heaven.*
*Oh! give me tidings that shall tell*
*When I may hope with Thee to dwell,*
*That I may quit this world of pain,*
*Nor seek to be its guest again.*
*A bird of holiness am I,*
*That from the vain world's net would fly;*
*Shed, bounteous Lord, one cheering shower*
*From Thy pure cloud of guiding power,*
*Before, even yet, the hour is come,*
*When my dust rises toward its home.*
*What are our deeds?—all worthless, all—*
*Oh, bring Devotion's wine,*
*That strength upon my soul may fall*
*From drops Thou mad'st divine.*
*The world's possessions fade and flee,*
*The only good is—loving Thee!*
*O happy hour! when I shall rise*
*From earth's delusions to the skies,*
*Shall find my soul at rest, and greet*
*The traces of my loved one's feet:*
*Dancing with joy, whirled on with speed,*
*Like motes that gorgeous sunbeams feed,*
*Until I reach the fountain bright*
*Whence yonder sun derives his light.*

**EARTHLY AND HEAVENLY LOVE**

*A being, formed like thee, of clay,*
*Destroys thy peace from day to day;*

*Excites thy waking hours with pain;*
*Consumes thy sleep with visions vain;*
*Thy mind is rapt, thy sense betrayed;*
*Thy head upon her foot is laid.*
*The teeming earth, the glowing sky,*
*Is nothing to her faintest sigh.*
*Thine eye sees only her; thy heart*
*Feels only her in every part.*
*Careless of censure, restless, lost,*
*By ceaseless wild emotions tossed;*
*If she demand thy soul, 'tis given—*
*She is thy life, thy death, thy heaven.*
*Since a vain passion, based on air,*
*Subdues thee with a power so rare,*
*How canst thou marvel those who stray*
*Tow'rd the true path are led away,*
*'Till, scarce the goal they can descry,*
*Whelmed in adoring mystery?*
*Life they regard not; for they live*
*In Him whose hands all being give:*
*The world they quit for Him, who made*
*Its wondrous light, its wondrous shade:*
*For Him all pleasures they resign,*
*And love Him with a love divine!*
*On the cupbearer gazing still,*
*The cup they break, the wine they spill.*
*From endless time their ears have rung*
*With words, by angel voices sung;*

*"Art thou not bound to God?" they cry;*
*And the blest "Yes" whole hosts reply.*
*They seem unmoved, but ceaseless thought*
*Works in their minds, with wisdom fraught.*
*Their feet are earth, but souls of flame*
*Dwell in each unregarded frame.*
*Such power by steady faith they gain,*
*One yell would rend the rocks in twain;*
*One word that cities could o'erthrow,*
*And spread abroad despair and woe.*
*Like winds, unseen, they rove all ways;*
*Silent, like stone, they echo praise:*
*So rapt, so blest, so filled are they,*
*They know not night—they see not day!*
*So fair He seems, all things who made,*
*The forms He makes to them are shade;*
*And, if a beauteous shape they view,*
*'Tis his reflection shining through.*
*The wise cast not the pearl away,*
*Charmed with the shell, whose hues are gay;*
*To him pure love is only known,*
*Who leaves both worlds for God alone.*

**THE DIVAN**

"Ala ya ayyuha's-Saki!"—*pass round and offer thou the bowl,*

*For love, which seemed at first so easy, has now brought trouble to my soul.*

*With yearning for the pod's aroma, which by the East that lock shall spread*

*From that crisp curl of musky odor, how plenteously our hearts have bled!*

*Stain with the tinge of wine thy prayer-mat, if thus the aged Magian bid,*

*For from the traveler from the Pathway no stage nor usage can be hid.*

*Shall my beloved one's house delight me, when issues ever and anon*

*From the relentless bell the mandate: A>Tis time to bind thy litters on"?*

*The waves are wild, the whirlpool dreadful, the shadow of the night steals o'er,*

*How can my fate excite compassion in the light-burdened of the shore?*

*Each action of my froward spirit has won me an opprobrious name;*

*Can any one conceal the secret which the assembled crowds proclaim?*

*If Joy be thy desire, O Hafiz,*

*From Him far distant never dwell.*

*"As soon as thou hast found thy Loved one,*

*Bid to the world a last farewell."*

*II*

*Thou whose features clearly beaming make the moon of Beauty bright,*

*Thou whose chin contains a well-pit which to Loveliness gives light.*

*When, O Lord! shall kindly Fortune, sating my ambition, pair*

*This my heart of tranquil nature and thy wild and ruffled hair?*

*Pining for thy sight my spirit trembling on my lip doth wait:*

*Forth to speed it, back to lead it, speak the sentence of its fate.*

*Pass me with thy skirt uplifted from the dusty bloody ground:*

*Many who have been thy victims dead upon this path are found.*

*How this heart is anguish-wasted let my heart's possessor know:*

*Friends, your souls and mine contemplate, equal by their common woe.*

*Aught of good accrues to no one witched by thy Narcissus eye:*

*Ne'er let braggart vaunt their virtue, if thy drunken orbs are nigh.*

*Soon my Fortune sunk in slumber shall her limbs with vigor brace:*

*Dashed upon her eye is water, sprinkled by thy shining face.*

*Gather from thy check a posy, speed it by the flying East;*

*Sent be perfume to refresh me from thy garden's dust at least.*

*Hafiz offers a petition, listen, and "Amen" reply:*

*"On thy sugar-dropping rubies let me for life's food rely."*

*Many a year live on and prosper, Sakis of the court of Jem,*

*E'en though I, to fill my wine-cup, never to your circle come.*

*East wind, when to Yazd thou wingest, say thou to its sons from me:*

*"May the head of every ingrate ball-like 'neath your mallbat be!"*

*"What though from your dais distant, near it by my wish I seem;*

*Homage to your Ring I render, and I make your praise my theme."*

*Shah of Shahs, of lofty planet, Grant for God what I implore;*

*Let me, as the sky above thee, Kiss the dust which strews thy floor.*

## V

*Up Saki!—let the goblet flow;*
*Strew with dust the head of our earthly woe!*
*Give me thy cup; that, joy-possessed,*
*I may tear this azure cowl from my breast.*
*The wise may deem me lost to shame,*
*But no care have I for renown or name.*
*Bring wine!—how many a witless head*
*By the wind of pride has with dust been spread!*
*My bosom's fumes, my sighs so warm,*
*Have inflamed yon crude and unfeeling swarm.*
*This mad heart's secret, well I know,*
*Is beyond the thoughts of both high and low.*
*E'en by that sweetheart charmed am I,*
*Who once from my heart made sweetness fly.*
*Who that my Silvern Tree hath seen,*
*Would regard the cypress that decks the green?*

*In grief be patient,*
*Night and day,*
*'Till thy fortune, Hafiz,*
*Thy wish obey.*

***VI***

*My heart no longer brooks my hand: sages, aid for God my woe!*

*Else, alas! my secret-deep soon the curious world must know.*

*The bark we steer has stranded: O breeze auspicious swell:*

*We yet may see once more the Friend we love so well.*

*The ten days' favor of the Sphere—magic is; a tale which lies.*

*Thou who wouldst befriend thy friends, seize each moment ere it flies.*

*At night, 'mid wine and flowers, the bulbul tuned his song:*

*"Bring thou the morning bowl: prepare, ye drunken throng!"*

*Sikander's mirror, once so famed, is the wine-filled cup: behold*

*All that haps in Dara's realm glassed within its wondrous mold.*

*O bounteous man, since Heaven sheds o'er thee blessings mild,*

*Inquire, one day at least, how fares Misfortune's child.*

*What holds in peace this twofold world, let this twofold sentence show:*

*"Amity to every friend, courtesy to every foe."*

*Upon the way of honor, impeded was my range;*
*If this affect thee, strive my destiny to change.*

*That bitter, which the Sufi styled "Mother of all woes that be,"*
*Seems, with maiden's kisses weighed, better and more sweet to me.*

*Seek drunkenness and pleasure 'till times of strait be o'er:*
*This alchemy of life can make the beggar Kore.*

*Submit; or burn thou taper-like e'en from jealousy o'ermuch:*
*Adamant, no less than wax, melts beneath that charmer's touch.*

*When fair ones talk in Persian, the streams of life outwell:*
*This news to pious Pirs, my Saki, haste to tell.*

*Since Hafiz, not by his own choice,*
*This his wine-stained cowl did win*
*Shaikh, who hast unsullied robes,*
*Hold me innocent of sin.*

*Arrayed in youthful splendor, the orchard smiles again;*
*News of the rose enraptures the bulbul of sweet strain.*

*Breeze, o'er the meadow's children, when thy fresh fragrance blows,*
*Salute for me the cypress, the basil, and the rose.*

*If the young Magian dally with grace so coy and fine,*
*My eye shall bend their fringes to sweep the house of wine.*

*O thou whose bat of amber hangs o'er a moon below,*

*Deal not to me so giddy, the anguish of a blow.*

*I fear that tribe of mockers who Lopers' ways impeach,*

*Will part with their religion the tavern's goal to reach.*

*To men of God be friendly: in Noah's ark was earth*

*Which deemed not all the deluge one drop of water worth.*

*As earth, two handfuls yielding, shall thy last couch supply,*

*What need to build thy palace, aspiring to the sky?*

*Flee from the house of Heaven, and ask not for her bread:*

*Her goblet black shall shortly her every guest strike dead.*

*To thee, my Moon of Canaan, the Egyptian throne pertains;*

*At length has come the moment that thou shouldst quit thy chains.*

*I know not what dark projects those pointed locks design,*

*That once again in tangles their musky curls combine.*

*Be gay, drink wine, and revel;*

*But not, like others, care,*

*O Hafiz, from the Qur'an*

*To weave a wily snare!*

***XII***

*Oh! where are deeds of virtue and this frail spirit where?*

*How wide the space that sunders the bounds of Here and There!*

*Can toping aught in common with works and worship own?*

*Where is regard for sermons, where is the rebec's Tone?*

*My heart abhors the cloister, and the false cowl its sign:*

*Where is the Magian's cloister, and where is his pure wine?*

*'Tis fled: may memory sweetly mind me of Union's days!*

*Where is that voice of anger, where those coquettish ways?*

*Can a foe's heart be kindled by the friend's face so bright?*

*Where is a lamp unlighted, and the clear Day-star's light?*

*As dust upon thy threshold supplies my eyes with balm,*

*If I forsake thy presence, where can I hope for calm?*

*Turn from that chin's fair apple; a pit is on the way.*

*To what, O heart, aspir'st thou? Whither thus quickly? Say!*

*Seek not, O friend, in Hafiz*

*Patience, nor rest from care:*

*Patience and rest—what are they?*

*Where is calm slumber, where?*

***XIV***

*At eve a son of song—his heart be cheerful long!—*

*Piped on his vocal reed a soul-inflaming lay.*

*So deeply was I stirred, that melody once heard,*
*That to my tearful eyes the things of earth grew gray.*
*With me my Saki was, and momently did he*
*At night the sun of Dai by lock and cheek display.*
*When he perceived my wish, he filled with wine the bowl*
*Then said I to that youth whose track was Fortune's way*
*"Saki, from Being's prison deliverance did I gain*
*When now and now the cup thou lit'st with cheerful ray.*
*"God guard thee here below from all the haps of woe;*
*God in the Seat of Bliss reward thee on His day!"*
*When Hafiz rapt has grown,*
*How, at one barleycorn,*
*Should he appraise the realm,*
*E'en of Kaus the Kay?*

***XVI***

*I said "O Monarch of the lovely, a stranger seeks thy grace this day."*
*I heard: "The heart's deceitful guidance inclines the stranger from his way."*
*Exclaimed I then: "One moment tarry!" "Nay," was the answer, "let me go;*
*How can the home-bred child be troubled by stories of a stranger's woe?"*
*Shall one who, gently nurtured, slumbers with royal ermine for a bed,*
*"Care if on rocks or thorns reposing the stranger rests his weary head?"*

*O thou whose locks hold fast on fetters so many a soul known long ago,*

*How strange that musky mole and charming upon thy cheek of vermil glow!*

*Strange is that ant-like down's appearance circling the oval of thy face;*

*Yet musky shade is not a stranger within the Hall which paintings grace.*

*A crimson tint, from wine reflected, gleams in that face of moonlight sheen;*

*E'en as the bloom of syrtis, strangely, o'er clusters of the pale Nasrin.*

*I said: "O thou, whose lock so night-black is evening in the stranger's sight,*

*Be heedful if, at break of morning, the stranger sorrow for his plight."*

*"Hafiz," the answer was, "familiars*

*Stand in amaze at my renown;*

*It is no marvel if a stranger*

*In weariness and grief sit down."*

***XVII***

*'Tis morn; the clouds a ceiling make:*

*The morn-cup, mates, the morn-cup take!*

*Drops of dew streak the tulip's cheek;*

*The wine-bowl, friends, the wine-bowl seek!*

*The greensward breathes a gale divine;*

*Drink, therefore, always limpid wine.*

*The Flower her emerald throne displays:*

*Bring wine that has the ruby's blaze.*

*Again is closed the vintner's store,*

*"Open, Thou Opener of the door!"*
*While smiles on us the season's boon,*
*I marvel that they close so soon.*
*Thy lips have salt-rights, 'tis confessed,*
*O'er wounds upon the fire-burnt breast.*
*Hafiz, let not*
*Thy courage fail!*
*Fortune, thy charmer*
*Shall unveil.*

### *XIX*

*Lo! from thy love's enchanting bowers Rizvan's bright gardens fresher grow;*

*From the fierce heat thine absence kindles, Gehenna's flames intenser glow.*

*To thy tall form and cheek resplendent, as to a place of refuge, fleet*

*Heaven and the Tuba-tree, and find there— "Happiness— and a fair retreat."*

*When nightly the celestial river glides through the garden of the skies,*

*As my own eye, it sees in slumber, naught but thy drunk narcissus eyes.*

*Each section of the spring-tiae's volume mares a fresh comment on thy name,*

*Each portal of the Empyrean murmurs the title of thy fame.*

*My heart has burned, but to ambition, the aim, still wished for, is denied:*

*These tears that tinged with blood are flowing, if I could reach it, would be dried.*

*What ample power thy salt-rights give thee (which both thy mouth and lips can claim),*

*Over a breast by sorrow wounded, and a heart burnt within its fame!*

*Oh! think not that the amorous only are drunk with rapture at thy sway:*

*Hast thou not heard of zealots, also, as reckless and as wrecked as they?*

*By thy lips' reign I hold it proven that the bright ruby's sheen is won*

*By the resplendent light that flashes out of a world-illuming sun.*

*Fling back thy veil! how long, oh tell me! shall drapery thy beauty pale?*

*This drapery, no profit bringing, can only for thy shame avail.*

*A fire within the rose's bosom was kindled when she saw thy face;*

*And soon as she inhaled thy fragrance, she grew all rose-dew from disgrace.*

*The love thy countenance awakens whelms Hafiz in misfortune's sea;*

*Death threatens him! ho there! give help, ere yet that he has ceased to be!*

*While life is thine, consent not, Hafiz,*
*That it should speed ignobly by;*
*But strive thou to attain the object*
*Of thy existence ere thou die.*

***XX***

*I swear—my master's soul bear witness, faith of old times, and promise leal!—*

*At early morning, my companion, is prayer for thy unceasing weal.*

*My tears, a more o'erwhelming deluge than was the flood which Noah braved,*

*Have washed not from my bosom's tablet the image which thy love has graved.*

*Come deal with me, and strike thy bargain: I have a broken heart to sell,*

*Which in its ailing state outvalues a hundred thousand which are well.*

*Be lenient, if thou deem me drunken: on the primeval day divine*

*Love, who possessed my soul as master, bent my whole nature unto wine.*

*Strive after truth that for thy solace the Sun may in thy spirit rise;*

*For the false dawn of earlier morning grows dark of face because it lies.*

*O heart, thy friend's exceeding bounty should free thee from unfounded dread;*

*This instant, as of love thou vauntest, be ready to devote thy head!*

*I gained from thee my frantic yearning for mountains and the barren plain,*

*Yet loath art thou to yield to pity, and loosen at mid-height my chain.*

*If the ant casts reproach on Asaf, with justice does her tongue upbraid,*

*For when his Highness lost Jem's signet, no effort for the quest he made.*

*No constancy—yet grieve not, Hafiz—*

*Expect thou from the faithless fair;*

*What right have we to blame the garden,*
*Because the plant has withered there?*

***XXII***

*Veiled in my heart my fervent love for him dwells,*
*And my true eye holds forth a glass to his spells.*
*Though the two worlds ne'er bowed my head when elate,*
*Favors as his have bent my neck with their weight.*
*Thine be the lote, but I Love's stature would reach.*
*Sigh like his zeal ascends the fancy of each.*
*Yet who am I that sacred temple to tread?*
*Still let the East that portal guard in my stead!*
*Spots on my robe—shall they arouse my complaint?*
*Nay! the world knows that he at least has no taint.*
*My turn has come; behold! Majnun is no more;*
*Five days shall fly, and each one's turn shall be o'er.*
*Love's ample realm, sweet joy, and all that is glad,*
*Save for his bounty I should never have had.*
*I and my heart—though both should sacrificed be,*
*Grant my friend's weal, their loss were nothing to me.*
*Ne'er shall his form within my pupil be dim,*
*For my eye's cell is but a chamber for him.*
*All the fresh blooms that on the greensward we view,*
*Gain but from him their scent and beauty of hue.*
*Hafiz seems poor;*
*But look within, for his breast,*
*Shrining his love,*
*With richest treasure is blest.*

### *XXIII*

*Prone at my friend's high gates, my Will its head lays still:*

*Whate'er my head awaits is ordered by that will.*

*My friend resembles none; in vain I sought to trace,*

*In glance of moon or sun, the radiance of that face.*

*Can morning's breeze make known what grief this heart doth hold,*

*Which as a bud hath grown, compressed by fold on fold?*

*Not I first drained the jar where rev'lers pass away:*

*Heads in this work-yard are naught else than wine-jars' clay.*

*Meseems thy comb has wreathed those locks which amber yield:*

*The gale has civet breathed, and amber scents the field.*

*Flowers of verdant nooks be strewn before thy face:*

*Let cypresses of brooks bear witness to thy grace!*

*When dumb grow tongues of men that on such love would dwell,*

*Why should a tongue-cleft pen by babbling strive to tell?*

*Thy cheek is in my heart; no more will bliss delay;*

*Glad omens e'er impart news of a gladder day.*

*Love's fire has dropped its spark*

*In Hafiz' heart before:*

*The wild-grown tulip's mark*

*Branded of old its core.*

### *XXV*

*Breeze of the morn, if hence to the land thou fliest—*
*Of my friend,*

*Return with a musky breath from the lock so sweet—*
*Of my friend.*

*Yea, by that life, I swear I would lay down mine in content,*

*If once I received through thee but a message sent—*
*Of my friend.*

*But—at that sacred court, if approach be wholly denied,*

*Convey, for my eyes, the dust that the door supplied—Of my friend.*

*I—but a beggar mean—can I hope for Union at last?*

*Ah! would that in sleep I saw but the shadow cast—*
*Of my friend.*

*Ever my pine-cone heart, as the aspen trembling and shy,*

*Has yearned for the pine-like shape and the stature high—Of my friend.*

*Not at the lowest price would my friend to purchase me care;*

*Yet I, a whole world to win, would not sell one hair—*
*Of my friend.*

*How should this heart gain aught,*

*Were its gyves of grief flung aside?*

*I, Hafiz, a bondsman, still*

*Would the slave abide—Of my friend.*

### *XXIX*

*Who of a Heaven on earth can tell, pure as the cell—*
*Of dervishes?*

*If in the highest state you'd dwell, be ever slaves—*
*Of dervishes.*

*The talisman of magic Might, hid in some ruin's lonely site,*
*Emerges from its ancient night at the wild glance—*
*Of dervishes.*

*When the proud sun has run his race, and he puts off his crown apace,*
*He bows before the pomp and place which are the boast—Of dervishes.*

*The palace portal of the sky, watched by Rizvan's unsleeping eye,*
*All gazers can at once descry from the glad haunts—*
*Of dervishes.*

*When mortal hearts are black and cold, that which transmutes them into gold*
*Is the alchemic stone we hold from intercourse—Of dervishes.*

*When tyranny, from pole to pole, sways o'er the earth with dire control,*
*We see from first to last unroll the victor-flag—Of dervishes.*

*There is a wealth which lasts elate, unfearful of decline from fate;*
*Hear it with joy—this wealth so great is in the hands—*
*Of dervishes.*

*Khosraus, the* kiblahs *of our prayer have weight to solace our despair,*
*But they are potent by their care for the high rank—*
*Of dervishes.*

*O, vaunter of thy riches' pride! lay all thy vanity aside,*

*And know that health and wealth abide but by the will—Of dervishes.*

*Korah lost all his treasured store, which, cursed of Heaven, sinks daily more,*

*(Hast thou not heard this tale of yore?) from disregard—Of dervishes.*

*The smiling face of joy unknown, yet sought by tenants of a throne,*

*Is only in the mirror shown of the clear face—Of dervishes.*

*Let but our Asaf's eye request, I am the slave of his behest,*

*For though his looks his rank attest, he has the mind—Of dervishes.*

*Hafiz, if of the tide thou think, which makes immortal those who drink,*

*Seek in the dust that fountain's brink, at the cell door—Of dervishes.*

*Hafiz, while here on earth, be wise:*

*He who to empire's rule would rise*

*Knows that his upward pathway lies*

*Through his regard—Of dervishes.*

***XXXI***

*In blossom is the crimson rose, and the rapt bulbul trills his song;*

*A summons that to revel calls you, O Sufis, wine-adoring throng!*

*The fabric of my contrite fervor appeared upon a rock to bide;*

*Yet see how by a crystal goblet it hath been shattered in its pride.*

*Bring wine; for to a lofty spirit, should they at its tribunal be,*

*What were the sentry, what the Sultan, the toper, or the foe of glee?*

*Forth from this hostel of two portals as finally thou needs must go,*

*What if the porch and arch of Being be of high span or meanly low?*

*To bliss' goal we gain not access, if sorrow has been tasted not;*

*Yea, with Alastu's pact was coupled the sentence of our baleful lot.*

*At Being and Non-being fret not; but either with calm temper see:*

*Non-being is the term appointed for the most lovely things that be.*

*Asaf's display, the airy courser, the language which the birds employed,*

*The wind has swept; and their possessor no profit from his wealth enjoyed.*

*Oh! fly not from thy pathway upward, for the winged shaft that quits the bow*

*A moment to the air has taken, to settle in the dust below.*

*What words of gratitude, O Hafiz*

*Shall thy reed's tongue express anon,*

*As its choice gems of composition*

*From hands to other hands pass on?*

### *XXXV*

*Now on the rose's palm the cup with limpid wine is brimming,*

*And with a hundred thousand tongues the bird her praise is hymning*

*Ask for a song-book, seek the wild, no time is this for knowledge;*

*The Comment of the Comments spurn, and learning of the college.*

*Be it thy rule to shun mankind, and let the Phoenix monish,*

*For the reports of hermit fame, from Kaf to Kaf astonish.*

*When yesterday our rector reeled, this sentence he propounded:*

*"Wine is a scandal; but far worse what men's bequests have founded."*

*Turbid or clear, though not thy choice, drink thankfully; well knowing*

*That all which from our Saki flows to his free grace is owing.*

*Each dullard who would share my fame, each rival self-deceiver,*

*Reminds me that at times the mat seems golden to its weaver.*

*Cease, Hafiz! store as ruddy gold*

*Thc wit that's in thy ditty:*

*The stampers of false coin, behold!*

*Are bankers for the city.*

***XLII***

*'Tis a deep charm which wakes the lover's flame,*

*Not ruby lip, nor verdant down its name.*

*Beauty is not the eye, lock, cheek, and mole;*

*A thousand subtle points the heart control.*

*XLIII*

*Zealot, censure not the toper, guileless though thou keep thy soul:*

*Certain 'tis that sins of others none shall write upon thy scroll.*

*Be my deeds or good or evil, look thou to thyself alone;*

*All men, when their work is ended, reap the harvest they have sown.*

*Never of Eternal Mercy preach that I must yet despair;*

*Canst thou pierce the veil, and tell me who is ugly, who is fair?*

*Every one the Friend solicits, be he sober, quaff he wine;*

*Every place has love its tenant, be it or the mosque, or shrine.*

*From the still retreat of virtue not the first am I to roam,*

*For my father also quitted his eternal Eden home.*

*See this head, devout submission: bricks at many a vintner's door:*

*If my foe these words misconstrue— "Bricks and head!" —Say nothing more.*

*Fair though Paradise's garden, deign to my advice to yield:*

*Here enjoy the shading willow, and the border of the field.*

*Lean not on thy store of merits; know'st thou 'gainst thy name for aye*

*What the Plastic Pen indited, on the Unbeginning Day?*

*Hafiz, if thou grasp thy beaker*
*When the hour of death is nigh,*
*From the street where stands the tavern*
*Straight they'll bear thee to the sky.*

***XLV***

*O breeze of morn! where is the place which guards my friend from strife?*

*Where is the abode of that sly Moon who lovers robs of life?*

*The night is dark, the Happy Vale in front of me I trace.*

*Where is the fire of Sinai, where is the meeting-place?*

*Here jointly are the wine-filled cup, the rose, the minstrel; yet*

*While we lack love, no bliss is here: where can my Loved be met?*

*Of the Shaikh's cell my heart has tired, and of the convent bare:*

*Where is my friend, the Christian's child, the vintner's mansion, where?*

*Hafiz, if o'er the glade of earth*
*The autumn-blast is borne,*
*Grieve not, but musing ask thyself:*
*"Where has the rose no thorn?"*

***LIX***

*My Prince, so gracefully thou steppest, that where thy footsteps fall—I'd die.*

*My Turk, so gracefully thou glidest, before thy stature tall—I'd die.*

*"When wilt thou die before me?"—saidst thou. Why thus so eagerly inquire?*

*These words of thy desire delight me; forestalling thy desire—I'd die.*

*I am a lover, drunk, forsaken: Saki, that idol, where is he?*

*Come hither with thy stately bearing! let me thy fair form see, —I'd die.*

*Should he, apart from whom I've suffered a life-long illness, day by day,*

*Bestow on me a glance, one only, beneath that orb dark-gray—I'd die.*

*"The ruby of my lips," thou saidst, "now bale, now balsam may exhale":*

*At one time from their healing balsam, at one time from their bale—I'd die.*

*How trim thy gait! May eye of evil upon thy face be never bent!*

*There dwells within my head this fancy; that at thy feet content—I'd die.*

*Though no place has been found for Hafiz*

*In Love's retreat, where hid thou art,*

*For me thine every part has beauty,*

*Before thine every part—I'd die.*

**LXIII**

*My heart has of the world grown weary and all that it can lend:*

*The shrine of my affection holds no Being but my friend.*

*If e'er for me thy love's sweet garden a fragrant breath exhale,*

*My heart, expansive in its joy, shall bud-like burst its veil.*

*Should I upon love's path advise thee, when now a fool I've grown,*

*'Twould be the story of the fool, the pitcher, and the stone.*

*Go! say to the secluded zealot: "Withhold thy blame; for know,*

*I find the arch of the* Mihrab *but in an eyebrow's bow."*

*Between the Kaaba and the wine-house, no difference I see*

*Whatever the spot my glance surveys, there equally is He.*

*'Tis not for beard, hair, eyebrow only, Kalandarism should care:*

*The Kalandar computes the Path by adding hair to hair.*

*The Kalandar who gives a hair's head,*<br>
*An easy path doth tread:*<br>
*The Kalandar of genuine stamp,*<br>
*As Hafiz gives his head.*

**LXIX**

*My heart desires the face so fair—Of Farrukh;*<br>
*It is perturbed as is the hair—Of Farrukh.*<br>
*No creature but that lock, that Hindu swart,*<br>
*Enjoyment from the cheek has sought—Of Farrukh.*<br>
*A blackmoor by Fortune blest is he,*<br>
*Placed at the side, and near the knee—Of Farrukh.*<br>
*Shy as the aspen is the cypress seen,*<br>
*Awed by the captivating mien—Of Farrukh.*<br>
*Saki, bring syrtis-tinted wine to tell*

*Of those narcissi, potent spell—Of Farrukh.*

*Bent as the archer's bow my frame is now,*

*From woes continuous as the brow—Of Farrukh.*

*E'en Tartar gales which musky odors whirl,*

*Faint at the amber-breathing curl—Of Farrukh.*

*If leans the human heart to any place,*

*Mine has a yearning to the grace—Of Farrukh.*

*That lofty soul*

*Shall have my service true,*

*That serves, as Hafiz,*

*The Hindu—Of Farrukh*

***LXXI***

*When now the rose upon the meadow from Nothing into Being springs,*

*When at her feet the humble violet with her head low in worship clings,*

*Take from thy morn-filled cup refreshment while tabors and the harp inspire,*

*Nor fail to kiss the chin of Saki while the flute warbles and the lyre.*

*Sit thou with wine, with harp, with charmer, until the rose's bloom be past;*

*For as the days of life which passes is the brief week that she shall last.*

*The face of earth, from herbal mansions, is lustrous as the sky; and shines*

*With asterisms of happy promise, with stars that are propitious signs.*

*In gardens let Zor'aster's worship again with all its rites revive,*

*While now within the tulip's blossoms the fires of Nimrod are alive.*

*Drink wine, presented by some beauty of Christ-like breath, of cheek fair-hued;*

*And banish from thy mind traditions to Ad relating, and Thamud.*

*Earth rivals the Immortal Garden during the rose and lily's reign;*

*But what avails when the immortal is sought for on this earth in vain?*

*When riding on the windy courser, as Solomon, the rose is found,*

*And when the Bird, at hour of morning, makes David's melodies resound,*

*Ask thou, in Solomon's dominion, a goblet to the brim renewed;*

*Pledge the Vizier, the cycle's Asaf, the column of the Faith, Mahmud.*

*O Hafiz, while his days continue, let joy eternal be thine aim;*

*And may the shadow of his kindness eternally abide the same!*

*Bring wine; for Hafiz, if in trouble,*
*Will ceaselessly the help implore*
*Of him who bounty shall aid ever,*
*As it has aid vouchsafed before.*

***LXXVII***

*Upon the path of Love, O heart, deceit and risk are great!*

*And fall upon the way shall he who at swift rate—Shall go.*

*Inflated by the wind of pride, the bubble's head may shine;*
*But soon its cap of rule shall fall, and merged in wine—Shall go.*

*O heart, when thou hast aged grown, shows airs of grace no more:*
*Remember that such ways as these when youth is o'er—Shall go.*

*Has the black book of black locks closed, the album yet shall stay,*
*Though many a score the extracts be which day by day—Shall go.*

***LXXXV***

*To me love's echo is the sweetest sound*
*Of all that 'neath this circling Round—Hath stayed.*

***LXXXVI***

*A beggar am I; yet enamored of one of cypress mold:*
*One in whose belt the hand bides only with silver and with gold.*

*Bring wine! let first the hand of Hafiz*
*The cheery cup embrace!*
*Yet only on one condition—*
*No word beyond this place!*

***LXXXVII***

*When beamed Thy beauty on creation's morn,*
*The world was set on fire by love new-born.*
*Thy cheek shone bright, yet angels' hearts were cold:*
*Then flashed it fire, and turned to Adam's mold.*
*The lamp of Reason from this fiame had burned,*
*But lightning jealousy the world o'erturned.*

*The enemy Thy secret sought to gain;*
*A hand unseen repelled the beast profane.*
*The die of Fate may render others glad:*
*My own heart saddens, for its lot is sad.*
*Thy chin's deep pit allures the lofty mind:*
*The hand would grasp thy locks in twines entwined.*
*Hafiz his love-scroll*
*To Thyself addressed,*
*When he had canceled*
*What his heart loved best.*

### *LXXXVIII*

*The preacher of the town will find my language hard, maybe:*
*While bent upon deceit and fraud, no Muslim is he.*
*Learn drinking and do gracious deeds; the merit is not great*
*If a mere brute shall taste not wine, and reach not man's estate.*
*Efficient is the Name Divine; be of good cheer, O heart!*
*The* div *becomes not Solomon by guile and cunning's art.*
*The benisons of Heaven are won by purity alone:*
*Else would not pearl and coral spring from every clod and stone?*

### *CI*

*Angels I saw at night knock at the wine-house gate:*
*They shaped the clay of Adam, flung into molds its weight.*
*Spirits of the Unseen World of Purities divine,*

*With me an earth-bound mortal, poured forth their 'wildering wine.*

*Heaven, from its heavy trust aspiring to be free,*

*The duty was allotted, mad as I am, to me.*

*Thank God my friend and I once more sweet peace have gained!*

*For this the houris dancing thanksgiving cups have drained.*

*With Fancy's hundred wisps what wonder that I've strayed,*

*When Adam in his prudence was by a grain betrayed?*

*Excuse the wrangling sects, which number seventy-two:*

*They knock at Fable's portal, for Truth eludes their view.*

*No fire is that whose flame the taper laughs to scorn:*

*True fire consumes to ashes the moth's upgarnered corn.*

*Blood fills recluses' hearts where Love its dot doth place,*

*Fine as the mole that glistens upon a charmer's face.*

*As Hafiz, none Thought's face*

*Hath yet unveiled; not e'en*

*Since for the brides of Language*

*Combed have their tresses been.*

***CXV***

*Lost Joseph shall return to Canaan's land—Despair not;*

*Affliction's cell of gloom with flowers shall bloom: Despair not.*

*Sad heart, thy state shall mend; repel despondency;*

*Thy head confused with pain shall sense regain: Despair not.*

*When life's fresh spring returns upon the dais mead,*

*O night-bird! o'er thy head the rose shall spread: Despair not.*

*Hope on, though things unseen may baffle thy research;*

*Mysterious sports we hail beyond the veil: Despair not.*

*Has the revolving Sphere two days opposed thy wish,*

*Know that the circling Round is changeful found: Despair not.*

*If on the Kaaba bent, thou brave the desert sand,*

*Though from the acacia's thorn thy foot be torn, Despair not.*

*Heart, should the flood of death life's fabric sweep away,*

*Noah shall steer the ark o'er billows dark: Despair not.*

*Though perilous the stage, though out of sight the goal,*

*Whithersoe'er we wend, there is an end: Despair not.*

*If Love evades our grasp, and rivals press our suit,*

*God, Lord of every change, surveys the range: Despair not.*

*Hafiz, in thy poor nook—*

*Alone, the dark night through—*

*Prayer and the Qur'an's page*

*Shall grief assuage—Despair not.*

## *CXXIX*

*Endurance, intellect, and peace have from my bosom flown,*

*Lured by an idol's silver ear-lobes, and its heart of stone.*

*An image brisk, of piercing looks, with peris' beauty blest,*

*Of slender shape, of lunar face, in Turk-like tunic drest!*

*With a fierce glow within me lit—in amorous frenzy lost—*

*A culinary pot am I, in ebullition tossed.*

*My nature as a shirt's would be, at all times free from smart,*

*If like yon tunic garb I pressed the wearer to my heart.*

*At harshness I have ceased to grieve, for none to light can bring*

*A rose that is apart from thorns, or honey void of sting.*

*The framework of this mortal form may rot within the mold,*

*But in my soul a love exists which never shall grow cold.*

*My heart and faith, my heart and faith—of old they were unharmed,*

*'Till by yon shoulders and yon breast, yon breast and shoulders charmed.*

*Hafiz, a medicine for thy woe,*<br>
*A medicine must thou sip,*<br>
*No other than that lip so sweet,*<br>
*That lip so sweet, that lip.*

## *CXXXIV*

*Although upon his moon-like cheek delight and beauty glow,*

*Nor constancy nor love is there: O Lord! these gifts bestow.*

*A child makes war against my heart; and he in sport one day*

*Will put me to a cruel death, and law shall not gainsay.*

*What seems for my own good is this: my heart from him to guard;*

*For one who knows not good from ill its guardianship were hard.*

*Agile and sweet of fourteen years that idol whom I praise:*

*His earrings in her soul retains the moon of fourteen days,*

*A breath as the sweet smell of milk comes from those sugary lips;*

*But from those black and roguish eyes behold what blood there drips!*

*My heart to find that new-born rose has gone upon its way;*

*But where can it be found, O Lord? I've lost it many a day.*

*If the young friend who owns my heart my center thus can break,*

*The Pasha will command him soon the lifeguard's rank to take.*

*I'd sacrifice my life in thanks,*

*If once that pearl of sheen*

*Would make the shell of Hafiz' eye*
*Its place of rest serene.*

*CXXXV*

*I tried my fortune in this city lorn:*
*From out its whirlpool must my pack be borne.*
*I gnaw my hand, and, heaving sighs of ire,*
*I light in my rent frame the rose's fire.*
*Sweet sang the bulbul at the close of day,*
*The rose attentive on her leafy spray:*
*"O heart! be joyful, for thy ruthless Love*
*Sits down ill-tempered at the sphere above.*
*"To make the false, harsh world thyself pass o'er,*
*Ne'er promise falsely and be harsh no more.*
*"If beat misfortune's waves upon heaven's roof,*
*Devout men's fate and gear bide ocean-proof.*
*"Hafiz, if lasting*
*Were enjoyment's day,*
*Jem's throne would never*
*Have been swept away."*

*CXLV*

*Breeze of the North, thy news allays my fears:*
*The hour of meeting with my Loved one nears.*
*Prospered by Heaven, O carrier pigeon, fly:*
*Hail to thee, hail to thee, come nigh, come nigh!*
*How fares our Salma? What Zu Salam's state?*
*Our neighbors there—are they unscathed by Fate?*
*The once gay banquet-hall is now devoid*
*Of circling goblets, and of friends who joyed.*

*Perished the mansion with its lot serene:*
*Interrogate the mounds where once 'twas seen.*
*The night of absence has now cast its shade:*
*What freaks by Fancy's night-gang will be played?*
*He who has loved relates an endless tale:*
*Here the most eloquent of tongues must fail.*
*My Turk's kind glances no one can obtain:*
*Alas, this pride, this coldness, this disdain!*
*In perfect beauty did thy wish draw nigh:*
*God guard thee from Kamal's malefic eye!*
*Hafiz, long will last*
*Patience, love, and pain?*
*Lovers' wail is sweet:*
*Do thou still complain.*

***CXLVI***

*O thou who has ravished my heart by thine exquisite grace and thy shape,*

*Thou carest for no one, and yet not a soul from thyself can escape.*

*At times I draw sighs from my heart, and at times, O my life, thy sharp dart:*

*Can aught I may say represent all the ills I endure from my heart?*

*How durst I to rivals commend thy sweet lips by the ruby's tent gemmed,*

*When words that are vivid in hue by a soul unrefined are contemned?*

*As strength to thy beauty accrues ev'ry day from the day sped before,*

*To features consummate as thine, will we liken the nightstar no more.*

*My heart hast thou reft: take my soul! For thine envoy of grief what pretense!*

*One perfect in grief as myself with collector as he may dispense.*

*O Hafiz, in Love's holy bane,*

*As thy foot has at last made its way,*

*Lay hold of his skirt with thy hand,*

*And with all sever ties from today.*

***CXLIX***

*Both worlds, the Transient and Eterne, for Saki and the Loved I'd yield:*

*To me appears Love's satellite the universe's ample field.*

*Should a new favorite win my place, my ruler shall be still supreme:*

*It were a sin should I my life more precious than my friend esteem.*

***CLV***

*Last night my tears, a torrent stream, stopped Sleep by force:*

*I painted, musing on thy down, upon the water-course.*

*Then, viewing my Beloved one's brow—my cowl burnt up—*

*In honor of the sacred Arch I drained my flowing cup.*

*From my dear friend's resplendent brow pure light was shed;*

*And on that moon there fell from far the kisses that I sped.*

*The face of Saki charmed my eye, the harp my ear:*

*At once for both mine ear and eye what omens glad were here!*

*I painted thine ideal face >till morning's light,*

*Upon the studio of my eye, deprived of sleep at night.*

*My Saki took at this sweet strain the wine-bowl up:*

*I sang to him these verses first; then drank to sparkling cup.*

*If any of my bird-like thoughts from joy's branch few,*

*Back from the springes of thy lock their fieeting wings I drew.*

*The time of Hafiz passed in joy*

*To friends I brought*

*For fortune and the days of life*

*The omens that they sought.*

***CLVII***

*Come, Sufi, let us from our limbs the dress that's worn for cheat Draw:*

*Let us a blotting line right through this emblem of deceit—Draw.*

*The convent's revenues and alms we'd sacrifice for wine awhile,*

*And through the vintry's fragrant flood this dervish-robe of guile—Draw.*

*Intoxicated, forth we'll dash, and from our feasting foe's rich stores*

*Bear off his wine, and then by force his charmer out of doors—Draw.*

*Fate may conceal her mystery, shut up within her hiding pale,*

*But we who act as drunken men will from its face the veil—Draw.*

*Here let us shine by noble deeds, lest we at last ashamed appear,*

*When starting for the other world, we hence our spirit's gear—Draw.*

*Tomorrow at Rizvan's green glade, should they refuse to make it ours,*

*We from their halls will the ghilrnam the houris from their bowers—Draw.*

*Where can we see her winking brow, that we, as the new moon of old,*

*At once may the celestial ball, as with a bat of gold, Draw?*

*O Hafiz! it becomes us not*
*Our boastful claims thus forth to put:*
*Beyond the limits of our rug*
*Why would we fain our foot—Draw?*

**CLIX**

*Aloud I say it, and with heart of glee:*
*"Love's slave am I, and from both worlds am free."*
*Can I, the bird of sacred gardens, tell*
*Into this net of chance how first I fell?*
*My place the Highest Heaven, an angel born,*
*I came by Adam to this cloister lorn.*
*Sweet houris, Tuba's shade, and Fountain's brink*
*Fade from my mind when of thy street I think.*
*Knows no astrologer my star of birth:*

*Lord, 'neath what plant bore me Mother Earth?*

*Since with ringed ear I've served Love's house of wine,*

*Grief's gratulations have each hour been mine.*

*My eyeball's man drains my heart's blood; 'tis just:*

*In man's own darling did I place my trust.*

*My Loved one's* Alif-*form stamps all my thought:*

*Save that, what letter has my master taught?*

*Let Hafiz' tear-drops*

*By thy lock be dried,*

*For fear I perish*

*In their rushing tide.*

***CLXVI***

*Knowest thou what fortune is?*

*'Tis Beauty's sight obtaining;*

*'Tis asking in her lane for alms,*

*And royal pomp disdaining.*

*Sev'rance from the wish for life an easy task is ever;*

*But lose we friends who sweeten life, the tie is hard to sever.*

*Bud-like with a serried heart I'll to the orchard wander;*

*The garment of my good repute I'll tear to pieces yonder;*

*Now, as doth the West-wind tell deep secrets to the Flower,*

*Hear now of Love's mysterious sport from bulbuls of the bower.*

*Kiss thy Beloved one's lips at first while the occasion lingers:*

*Await thou else disgust at last from biting lip and fingers.*

*Profit by companionship: this two-doored house forsaken,*

*No pathway that can thither lead in future time is taken.*

*Hafiz from the thought, it seems,*

*Of Shah Mansur has fleeted;*

*O Lord! remind him that the poor*

*With favor should be treated.*

### *CLXXIII*

*With my heart's blood I wrote to one most dear:*

*"The earth seems doom-struck if thou art not near.*

*"My eyes a hundred signs of absence show:*

*These tears are not their only signs of woe."*

*I gained no boon from her for labor spent:*

*"Who tries the tried will in the end repent."*

*I asked how fared she; the physician spake:*

*"Afar from her is health; but near her ache."*

*The East-wind from my Moon removed her veil:*

*At morn shone forth the Sun from vapors pale.*

*I said: "They'll mock, if I go round thy lane."*

*By God! no love escapes the mocker's bane.*

*Grant Hafiz' prayer:*

*"One cup, by life so sweet!"*

*He seeks a goblet*

*With thy grace replete!*

## *CLXXX*

*O thou who art unlearned still, the quest of love essay:*

*Canst thou who hast not trod the path guide others on the way?*

*While in the school of Truth thou stay'st, from Master Love to learn,*

*Endeavor, though a son today, the father's grade to earn.*

*Slumber and food have held thee far from Love's exalted good:*

*Wouldst thou attain the goal of love, abstain from sleep and food.*

*If with the rays of love of truth thy heart and soul be clear,*

*By God! thy beauty shall outshine the sun which lights the sphere.*

*Wash from the dross of life thy hands, as the Path's men of old,*

*And winning Love's alchemic power, transmute thyself to gold.*

*On all thy frame, from head to foot, the light of God shall shine,*

*If on the Lord of Glory's path nor head nor foot be thine.*

*An instant plunge into God's sea, nor e'er the truth forget*

*That the Seven Seas' o'erwhelming tide, no hair of thine shall wet.*

*If once thy glancing eye repose on the Creator's face,*

*Thenceforth among the men who glance shall doubtless be thy place.*

*When that which thy existence frames all upside-down shall be,*
*Imagine not that up and down shall be the lot of thee.*
*Hafiz, if ever in thy head*
*Dwell Union's wish serene,*
*Thou must become the threshold's dust*
*Of men whose sight is keen.*

# 9

## JOSEPH AND ZULEIKA

*Jami, the last of the great classic poets of Persia, was born at Jam, near Herat, in 1414 and died in Herat in 1492. He essayed every form of literature and achieved success in each. From childhood he was welcomed everywhere as a marvel of brilliancy. He himself wrote that he never found a master who knew more than he. When we seek for the work which best represents this universal genius, we find it perhaps in his chief love-tale, which follows below. This mingles Nizami's romantic touch with Jalal's Sufism and the fire of Hafiz. It is Jami at his highest note.*

*Zuleika, the daughter of Taimus, King of Mauretania, beheld in a dream a figure of such extraordinary beauty that she became immediately enamored of the glorious vision, and sank into a deep melancholy, fruitlessly longing for the unknown object. This dream was three times repeated, and the last time the beautiful apparition named Egypt as the land of his abode. He is indeed Joseph, or Yusuf, of the Old Testament, and Zuleika is to play the part of Potiphar's wife. The following is abridged by L. M. Costello.*

The ravens of the night were hushed,
The bird of dawn began his lay,
The rosebud, newly awakened, blushed
To feel the touch of springing day,
And bade the roses round unveil,
Roused by the warbling nightingale.
The jasmine stood all bathed in dew;

Wet were the violet's lids of blue.
Zuleika, fairer than the flowers,
Lay tranced—for 'twas not sleep that stole
Her senses, through the night's still hours,
And raised new visions to her soul.
The heart unfettered, free to rove,
Turned toward the idol of her love.
No—'twas not sleep, 'twas motionless,
Unbroken thought, repressed in vain;
The shadow of the day's distress,
A frenzy of remembered pain.
But, 'midst those pangs, what rapture still;
The same dear form is ever there;
Those eyes the rays of Eden fill
And odors of the blest distill
From every curl of that bright hair!
His smiles!—such smiles as *houris* wear
When from their caves of pearl they come,
And bid the true believer share
The pleasures of their sacred home.
See, on his shoulder shines a star
That glows and dazzles as he moves:
She feels its influence afar,
She gazes, worships, hopes—and loves!

*At this period, while her mind is absorbed by the one engrossing idea, an embassy arrives in Mauritania from that very country, Egypt, the land of all her hopes, soliciting the hand of the princess for the Asis, or grand vizier of Pharaoh, an offer which she unhesitatingly accepts, being secretly convinced that her visionary lover and her proposed future husband are the same. She accordingly departs for Egypt, with a splendid and numerous retinue, and makes a magnificent entry into Memphis, under the escort of the Asis Potiphar, or*

*Kitfir, himself, who comes to meet his bride. Curious to discover his identity, she anxiously seizes an opportunity of peeping through the curtains of her litter, but is filled with grief and dismay on finding a totally different person from the lovely image of her dreams. She thus exclaims, on hearing the acclamations which announce the arrival of the Asis, when he first comes to meet her, before she has yet made the discovery fatal to her peace:*

O joy too great!—O hour too blest!
He comes—they hail him—now, more near,
His eager courser's feet I hear.
Oh heart! be hushed within my breast,
Burst not with rapture! Can it be?
The idol of my life—divine,
All radiant, clothed in mystery,
And loving me as I adore,
As none dared ever love before,
Shall be—nay, is—even now, is mine!
I will be patient, but his breath
Seems stealing o'er my senses—death
Were better than suspense like this—
One draught—though 'twere the last—of bliss!
One glance, though in that glance I die,
To prove the glorious certainty!
Not he! not he! on whom for years
My soul has dwelt with sacred truth;
For whom my life has passed in tears,
And wasted was my bloom of youth;
For whom I breathed, and thought, and moved,
My own, my worshiped, my beloved!
I hailed the night, that I might gaze
Upon his star's unconquered blaze:
The morn but rose that I might pray,

Hope, wish, expect from day to day,
My sole existence was that thought,
And I do wake to know 'tis naught?
Vain tears, vain madness, vain endeavor,
Another blasts my sight forever !
Dawn upon the wide world broke,
And the sun's warm rays awoke;
Scattering o'er the cloudy sky
Hues of rich variety:
Such bright tinting as illumes
With its rays the peacock's plumes,
And the parrot's feathers bright,
Touches with a starry light.
The Asis rides in kingly guise;
Yon curtained litter holds the prize
More precious than all wealth beside—
His own, his young, his peerless bride.
Around, afar, of homage proud,
In countless ranks his warriors crowd,
Well may the lordly Asis boast
The glories of his gorgeous host.
Rich are the veils, profusely spread,
That canopy the "fair one's" head;
Like some delicious tree that throws
Its shade, inviting to repose:
And, like soft turf, the carpets lie,
Bedecked with gay embroidery.
The temple moves, all-glorious, on—
Throned in the midst the "happy one."
All heaven resounds with shout and song,
As the bright pageant sweeps along.
The camel-drivers' cries succeed,

Urging their stately beasts to speed.
Whose hoofs, with swift and frequent tread,
The sands with moonlike forms have spread:
The earth is plowed with coursers' feet
And still fresh hosts the wounds repeat.
Many a fair and blushing maid
Exulted in the gay parade:
And all who called the Asis lord
Hailed the fair idol he adored.
But she— "the beautiful," "the blest"—
What pangs, what tumults shook her breast!
She sat, concealed from every eye—
Alone—in hopeless misery.
"O Fate!" she cried; "O ruthless Fate!
Why am I made thy mark of hate?
Why must my heart thy victim be?
Thus lost, abandoned—crushed by thee!
Thou camest, in troubled dreams, and stole
The peace, the pleasure of my soul,
In visions that the blest might share,
Whose only fruit has been despair.
I see each glittering fabric fall;
But vain reproach, vain trust, vain all!
For help, for rest, where can I fly?
My heart is riven—let me die!
Have I then lingered long in pain,
In sad suspense, in musings vain,
To be—O crowning grief! betrayed,
In foreign lands a victim made?
Relentless destiny! accurst
Were all the joys thy visions nurst.
Is there no drop of hope left yet?

Must I all promises forget?
Dash not my cup to earth: say, Power benign,
I may be blest—even yet he may be mine!"
"Why hast thou thus cruelly
Robbed me of my peace?
What have I done to thee to be thus treated;
it is folly indeed that I seek help from thee.
When souls melt, thou art called upon for aid;
What is the melting of thy soul?"
Thus raved Zuleika, when without
Arose the sudden deafening shout
That hailed the close of all their toil—
"Lo!—Memphis! and the banks of Nile!"
Then, far and ide, the glittering ranks
Rush to the fiowery river's banks.
The Asis' sign his slaves obey,
Gold, silver, flowers, bestrew the way:
And o'er the litter gems are thrown,
Whose countless rays like meteors shone;
As thick they fall as on the rose
Hang the rich dews at evening's close;
The courser's feet on rubies trod,
O'er mounds of gold the camel strode.
On swept the train—one gorgeous mile,
Planting with gems the banks of Nile;
The proud stream rolled its waters deep
O'er pearls in many a shining heap:
Each shell was filled with pearls; each scale
That clothed the crocodile in mail
Was changed to silver, as he lay
And basked amidst the fervid ray.
And onward to the palace-gate

The train poured on, in sumptuous state;
The glowing portals opened wide—
In flowed the overwhelming tide,
Ushering the Asis and his bride.
A throne the Peris might have framed,
The sun and moon's pale luster shamed:
And she, whose radiance all effaced—
Zuleika—on the throne was placed.
Sparkling with jewels, red with gold,
Her heart shrunk, withered, crushed, and cold;
Although a feverish sense of pain
Frenzied her mind and seared her brain:
As on a flaming hearth she sat—
Amidst rejoicing—desolate!
Laden with many a priceless gem,
Crowned with a gorgeous diadem.
Each pearl a poisonous drop appears:
And from her eyes fall scalding tears.
And thus a crown is gained—for this,
We leave all thoughts of present bliss!
We toil, we strive, we live in care,
And in the end possess—despair!
Our sun of youth, of hope, is set,
And all our guerdon is—regret!

The poem now pursues the Scriptural account of the life of Joseph, or Yussuf, whose supernatural beauty is, however, described as being the especial gift of God, and recorded to have been so great that no woman could look on him without love. Zuleika, therefore, only shared the fate of all her sex. Some writers say the ladies who clamored so much against her for her passion were, when he first entered the chamber where they were all assembled, in the act of cutting pomegranates, some say oranges, and in their admiration and amazement cut their fingers instead of the fruit! Yussuf is considered the emblem of divine perfection, and Zuleika's love is the image of the love of the creature toward the Creator: some go so far as to say that we ought to follow her example, and should permit the beauty of God to transport us out of ourselves. The rapid change from prison to high estate of Yussuf they consider a type of the impatience of the soul to burst its fetters and join its Creator.

*Yussuf was always surrounded with a celestial light, typical as well of the moral beauty and wisdom which adorned his mind. He is sold as a slave, and Zuleika becomes his purchaser, to the great rage and envy of all her rivals, amongst whom was included the Princess Nasigha, of the race of Aad. The beautiful Yussuf now enters her service, and, at his own desire, a flock of sheep are given to his special keeping, his admiring mistress wishing, by every indulgence, to attach him to her. The nurse of Zuleika is the confidante of the passion which she cannot control, and which, at length, in an imprudent moment, she discloses to its object himself. His father, Jacob, or the angel Gabriel in his likeness, appears, to warn him of his danger, and he flies, leaving his mistress in an agony of despair, rage, and grief. She thus exclaims:*

Is this a dream?—another dream,
Like that which stole my senses first,
Which sparkled o'er my life's dull stream,
By idle, erring fancy nursed?
Was it for this my life I spent
In murmurs deep, and discontent—
Slighted, for this, all homage due,
From gen'rous, faithful love withdrew?
For this, no joy, no pomp have prized;
For this, all honors have despised—
Left all my soul, to passion free,
To be thus hated—spurned-by thee?
O God! to see thee loathing turn,

While on my cheeks swift blushes burn:
Contempt, abhorrence on thy brow,
Where radiant sweetness dwelt—>till now!
Thy bitter accents, fierce, severe,
In harsh, unwonted tones to hear:
Thy horror, thy disgust to view,
And know thy accusations true!
All, all but this I could have borne—
A husband's vengeance and his scorn;
To be reproached, disgraced, reviled,
So Yussuf on his victim smiled.
I would, amidst the desert's gloom,
Have hailed, with thee, a living tomb;
My home, my state, my birth forgot,
And, with thy love, embraced thy lot;
Had taught my heart all pangs to share,
And prove what perfect love can dare.
Let me look back to that dark hour
That bound my spirit to thy power—
Thy grateful words, thy glance recall,
My hopes, my love—and curse them all;
Let me thy tender looks retrace,
The glories of thy heavenly face;
Thy brow, where Aden's splendor lies,
And the mild luster of thine eyes:
Yet, let my heart no weakness prove,
But hate thee as I once could love.
What fearful eloquence was thine,
What awful anger—just—divine!
Shuddering, I saw my heart displayed.
And knew all this I should have said!
'Twas mine to shrink, withstand, in time,

For, while I sinned, I knew my crime.
O wretched, wavering heart!—as vain
Thy wild resentment as thy pain:
One thought alone expels the rest,
One sole regret distracts my breast,
O'ermastering and subduing all—
More than my crime, more than my fall:
Are not shame, fear, remorse, forgot,
In that one thought—he loves me not?
Though in a dark and narrow cell
The "fair beloved" confined may dwell,
No prison is that dismal place,
'Tis filled with dignity and grace:
And the damp vaults and gloom around
Are joyous spring, with roses crowned.
Not Paradise to me were fair
If he were not a dweller there;
Without his presence all is night,
My soul awakes but in his sight:
Though this frail tenement of clay
May here amidst its pomp remain,
My spirit wanders far away,
And dwells with his in prisoned pain.
In solitude, where Being signless dwelt,
And all the universe still dormant lay
Concealed in selflessness, One Being was
Exempt from "I" or "Thou"-ness, and apart
From all duality; Beauty Supreme,
Unmanifest, except unto Itself
By Its own light, yet fraught with power to charm
The souls of all; concealed in the Unseen,
An Essence pure, unstained by aught of ill.

No mirror to reflect Its loveliness,
Nor comb to touch Its locks; the morning breeze
Ne'er stirred Its tresses; no collyrium
Lent luster to Its eyes; no rosy cheeks
O'ershadowed by dark curls like hyacinth
Nor peach-like down were there; no dusky mole
Adorned Its face; no eye had yet beheld
Its image. To Itself it sang of Love
In wordless measures. By Itself it cast
The die of Love. But Beauty can not brook
Concealment and the veil, nor patient rest
Unseen and unadmired; 'twill burst all bonds,
And from Its prison-casement to the world
Reveal Itself. See where the tulip grows
In upland meadows, how in balmy spring
It decks itself; and how amidst its thorns
The wild rose rends its garment, and reveals
Its loveliness. Thou too, when some rare thought;
Or beauteous image, or deep mystery
Flashes across thy soul, canst not endure
To let it pass, but holdst it, that perchance
In speech or writing thou mayst send it forth
To charm the world. Whatever beauty dwells,
Such is its nature, and its heritage
From Everlasting Beauty, which emerged
From realms of purity to shine upon
The worlds, and all the souls which dwell therein.
One gleam fell from It on the universe
And on the angels, and this single ray
Dazzled the angels, till their senses whirled
Like the revolving sky. In diverse forms
Each mirror showed it forth, and everywhere

Its praise was chanted in new harmonies.
The cherubim, enraptured, sought for songs
Of praise. The spirits who explore the depths
Of boundless seas, wherein the heavens swim
Like some small boat, cried with one mighty voice,
"Praise to the Lord of all the universe!"
Behold those spheres forever circling, bound
With scarves of azure, in their mystic round.
See, their light mantles loosely floating throw
A flood of radiance on the world below.
See them pursuing through the night and day,
True to their purpose, their triumphant way.
Each, like a player's ball obedient, still
Is moved and guided by superior will.
One eastward from the west its journey bends,
The other's ship to western waves descends.
Each in due progress with alternate sway
Lights the still night or cheers the busy day.
One writes fair lines that promise golden joys:
One with sad aspect bonds of bliss destroys.
All, joying in their might, their task renew,
And with untiring haste their course pursue.
Onward forever to the goal they press
With feet and loins that know not weariness.
Who learns the secret of their dark intent?
Who knows on whom each wanderer's face is bent?
No heart is that which love ne'er wounded: they
Who know not lovers' pangs are soulless clay.
Turn from the world, O turn thy wandering feet;
Come to the world of Love and find it sweet.
Once to his master a disciple cried:
"To wisdom's pleasant path be thou my guide."

"East thou ne'er loved?" the master answered; "learn
The ways of love and then to me return."
Drink deep of earthly love, that so thy lip
May learn the wine of holier love to sip.
But let not form too long thy soul entrance:
Pass o'er the bridge; with rapid feet advance.
If thou wilt rest, thine ordered journey sped,
Forbear to linger at the bridge's head.
In this orchestra full of vain deceit
The drum of Being, each in turn, we beat.
Each morning brings new truth to light and fame,
And on the world falls luster from a name.
If in one constant course the ages rolled,
Full many a secret would remain untold.
If the sun's splendor never died away,
Ne'er would the market of the stars be gay.
If in our gardens endless frost were king,
No rose would blossom at the kiss of Spring
Her face was the garden of Iram, where
Roses of every hue are fair.
The dusky moles that enhanced the red
Were like Moorish boys playing in each rose-bed.
Of silver that paid no tithe, her chin
Had a well with the Water of Life therein.
If a sage in his thirst came near to drink,
He would feel the spray ere he reached the brink,
But lost were his soul if he nearer drew,
For it was a well and a whirlpool too.
Her neck was of ivory. Thither drawn,
Came with her tribute to beauty the fawn;
And the rose hung her head at the gleam of the skin
Of shoulders fairer than jasmine.

Her breasts were orbs of a light most pure,
Twin bubbles new-risen from fount Kafur,
Two young pomegranates grown on one spray,
Where bold hope never a finger might lay.
The touchstone itself was proved false when it tried
Her arms' fine silver thrice purified;
But the pearl-pure amulets fastened there
Were the hearts of the holy absorbed in prayer.
"I shall roll up the carpet of life when I see
Thy dear face again, and shall cease to be,
For self will be lost in that rapture, and all
The threads of my thought from my hand will fall;
Not me wilt thou find, for this self will have fled:
Thou wilt be my soul in mine own soul's stead.
All thought of self will be swept from my mind,
And thee, only thee, in my place shall I find;
More precious than heaven, than earth more dear,
Myself were forgotten if thou wert near."
"Mine eyes have been touched by the Truth's pure ray,
And the dream of folly has passed away.
Mine eyes thou hast opened—God bless thee for it!—
And my heart to the Soul of the soul thou hast knit.
From a fond strange love thou hast turned my feet
The Lord of all creatures to know and meet;
If I bore a tongue in each single hair, Each and all should thy praise declare."
"By the excellent bloom of that cheek which He gave,
By that beauty which makes the whole world thy slave;
By the splendor that beams from that beautiful brow,
That bids the full moon to thy majesty bow;
By the graceful gait of that cypress, by
The delicate bow that is bent o'er thine eye;

By that arch of the temple devoted to prayer,
By each fine-woven mesh of the coils of thy hair;
By that charming narcissus, that form arrayed
In the sheen and glory of silk brocade;
By that secret thou callest a mouth, by the hair
Thou callest the waist of that body most fair;
By the musky spots on thy cheek's pure rose,
By the smile of thy lips when those buds unclose;
By my longing tears, by the sigh and groan
That rend my heart as I pine alone;
By thine absence, a mountain too heavy to bear,
By my thousand fetters of grief and care;
By the sovereign sway of my passion,
By thy carelessness whether I live or die;
Pity me, pity my lovelorn grief:
Loosen my fetters and grant relief:
An age has scorched me since over my soul
The soft sweet air of thy garden stole.
Be the balm of my wounds for a little; shed
Sweet scent on the heart where the flowers are dead.
I hunger for thee till my whole frame is weak:
O give me the food for my soul which I seek."
In his stalls had Yussuf a fairy steed,
A courser through space of no earthly breed;
Swift as the heavens, and black and white
With a thousand patches of day and night;
Now a jetty spot, now a starry blaze,
Like Time with succession of nights and days.
With his tail the heavenly Virgo's hair,
With his hoof the moon was afraid to compare.
Each foot with a golden new moon was shod,
And the stars of its nails struck the earth as he trod.

When his hoof smote sharp on the rugged flint
A planet flashed forth from the new moon's dint;
And a new moon rose in the sky when a shoe
From the galloping foot of the courser flew.
Like an arrow shot through its side in the chase,
He outstripped the game in the deadly race.
At a single bound he would spring, unpressed,
With the lightning's speed from the east to the west.
"O thou who hast broken mine honor's urn,
Thou stone of offense wheresoever I turn,
I should smite—for thy falsehood has ruined my rest—
with the stone thou art made of, the heart in my breast.
The way of misfortune too surely I trod
When I bowed down before thee and made thee my god;
When I looked up to thee with wet eyes in my woe,
I renounced all the bliss which both worlds can bestow.
From thy stony dominion my soul will I free,
And thus shatter the gem of thy power and thee."
With a hard flint stone like the Friend, as she spoke,
In a thousand pieces the image she broke.
Riven and shattered the idol fell,
And with her from that moment shall all be well.
She made her ablution, 'mid penitent sighs,
With the blood of her heart and the tears of her eyes.
She bent down her head to the dust; with a moan
She made supplication to God's pure throne:
"O God, who lovest the humble,
Thou To whom idols, their makers, their servants bow;
'Tis to the light which Thy splendor lends
To the idol's face that its worshiper bends.
Thy love the heart of the sculptor stirs,
And the idol is graven for worshipers.

They bow them down to the image, and think
That they worship Thee as before it they sink.
To myself, O Lord, I have done this wrong,
If mine eyes to an idol have turned so long.
Thou hast washed the dark stain of my sin away;
Now restore the lost blessing for which I pray.
May I feel my heart free from the brand of its woes,
And cull from the garden of Yussuf a rose."
"Where is thy youth, and thy beauty, and pride?"
"Gone, since I parted from thee!" she replied.
"Where is the light of thine eye?" said he,
"Drowned in blood-tears for the loss of thee."
"Why is that cypress-tree bowed and bent?"
"By absence from thee and my long lament."
"Where is thy pearl, and thy silver and gold,
And the diadem bright on thy head of old?"
"She who spoke of my loved one," she answered, "shed,
In the praise of thy beauty, rare pearls on my head.
In return for those jewels, a recompense meet,
I scattered my jewels and gold at her feet.
A crown of pure gold on her forehead I set,
And the dust that she trod was my coronet.
The stream of my treasure of gold ran dry;
My heart is Love's storehouse, and I am I."
"Not love thee!—ah! how much I loved
Long absent years of grief have proved.
Severe rebuke, assumed disdain,
Dwelt in my words and looks in vain:
I would not passion's victim be,
And turned from sin—but not from thee.
My love was pure, no plant of earth
From my rapt being sprung to birth:

I loved as angels might adore,
And sought, and wished, and hoped no more.
Virtue was my belov'd: and thou
Hadst virtue's impress on thy brow.
Thy weakness showed how frail is all
That erring mortals goodness call.
I thanked thee, and reproached thee not
For all the sufferings of my lot.
The God we worship was thy friend,
And led me to my destined end,
Taught the great lesson to thy heart
That vice and bliss are wide apart:
And joined us now, that we may prove
With perfect virtue, perfect love.
The beauty returned which was ruined and dead,
And her cheek gained the splendor which long had fled.
Again shone the waters which sad years had dried,
And the rose-bed of youth bloomed again in its pride.
The musk was restored and the camphor withdrawn,
And the black night followed the gray of the dawn.
The cypress rose stately and tall as of old:
The pure silver was free from all wrinkle and fold.
From each musky tress fled the traces of white:
To the black narcissus came beauty and light.
"The one sole wish of my heart," she replied,
"Is still to be near thee, to sit by thy side;
To have thee by day in my happy sight,
And to lay my cheek on thy foot at night;
To lie in the shade of the cypress and sip
The sugar that lies on thy ruby lip;
To my wounded heart this soft balm to lay;
For naught beyond this can I wish or pray.

The streams of thy love will new life bestow
On the dry thirsty field where its sweet waters flow."
Thus spoke the Angel: "To thee, O King,
From the Lord Almighty a message I bring:
Mine eyes have seen her in humble mood;
I heard her prayer when to thee she sued.
At the sight of her labors, her prayers, and sighs,
The waves of the sea of my pity rise.
Her soul from the sword of despair I free,
And here from My throne I betroth her to thee."

## 10

# The Rubaiyat

*1.*

*At dawn a cry through all the tavern shrilled,*
*"Arise, my brethren of the revelers' guild,*
*That I may fill our measure full of wine,*
*Or e'er the measure of our days be filled."*

*2.*

*Who was it brought thee here at nightfall, who?*
*Forth from the harem in this manner, who?*
*To him who in thy absence burns as fire,*
*And trembles like hot air, who was it, who?*

*3.*

*'Tis but a day we sojourn here below,*
*And all the gain we get is grief and woe,*
*Then, leaving our life's riddles all unsolved,*
*And burdened with regrets, we have to go.*

*4.*

*Khaja! grant one request, and only one,*
*Wish me God-speed, and get your preaching done;*
*I walk aright, 'tis you who see awry;*
*Go! heal your purblind eyes, leave me alone.*

**5.**

*Arise! and come, and of thy courtesy*
*Resolve my weary heart's perplexity,*
*And fill my goblet, so that I may drink,*
*Or e'er they make their goblets out of me.*

**6.**

*When I am dead, with wine my body lave,*
*For obit chant a bacchanalian stave,*
*And, if you need me at the day of doom,*
*Beneath the tavern threshold seek my grave.*

**7.**

*Since no one can assure thee of the morrow,*
*Rejoice thy heart to-day, and banish sorrow*
*With moonbright wine, fair moon, for heaven's moon*
*Will look for us in vain on many a morrow.*

**8.**

*Let lovers all distraught and frenzied be,*
*And flown with wine, and reprobates, like me;*
*When sober, I find everything amiss,*
*But in my cups cry, "Let what will be, be."*

**9.**

*In Allah's name, say, wherefore set the wise*
*Their hearts upon this house of vanities?*
*Whene'er they think to rest them from their toils,*
*Death takes them by the hand, and says, "Arise."*

**10.**

*Men say the Koran holds all heavenly lore,*
*But on its pages seldom care to pore;*

*The lucid lines engraven on the bowl—*
*That is the text they dwell on evermore.*

**11.**

*Blame not the drunkards, you who wine eschew,*
*Had I but grace, I would abstain like you,*
*And mark me, vaunting zealot, you commit*
*A hundredfold worse sins than drunkards do.*

**12.**

*What though 'tis fair to view, this form of man,*
*I know not why the heavenly Artizan*
*Hath set these tulip cheeks and cypress forms*
*To deck the mournful halls of earth's divan.*

**13.**

*My fire gives forth no smoke-cloud here below,*
*My stock-in-trade no profit here below,*
*And you, who call me tavern-haunter, know*
*There is indeed no tavern here below.*

**14.**

*Thus spake an idol to his worshiper,*
*"Why dost thou worship this dead stone, fair sir?*
*'Tis because He who gazeth through thine eyes*
*Doth some part of His charms on it confer. "*

**15.**

*Whate'er thou doest, never grieve thy brother,*
*Nor kindle fumes of wrath his peace to smother;*
*Dost thou desire to taste eternal bliss,*
*Vex thine own heart, but never vex another!*

***16.***

*O Thou! to please whose love and wrath as well,*
*Allah created heaven and likewise hell;*
*Thou hast thy court in heaven, and I have naught,*
*Why not admit me in thy courts to dwell?*

***17.***

*So many cups of wine will I consume,*
*Its bouquet shall exhale from out my tomb,*
*And every one that passes by shall halt,*
*And reel and stagger with that mighty fume.*

***18.***

*Young wooer, charm all hearts with lover's art,*
*Glad winner, lead thy paragon apart!*
*A hundred Kaabas equal not one heart,*
*Seek not the Kaaba, rather seek a heart!*

***19.***

*What time, my cup in hand, its draughts I drain,*
*And with rapt heart unconsciousness attain,*
*Behold what wondrous miracles are wrought—*
*Songs flow as water from my burning brain.*

***20.***

*To-day is but a breathing space, quaff wine!*
*Thou wilt not see again this life of thine;*
*So, as the world becomes the spoil of time,*
*Offer thyself to be the spoil of wine!*

***21.***

*'Tis we who to wine's yoke our necks incline,*
*And risk our lives to gain the smiles of wine;*

*The henchman grasps the flagon by its throat*
*And squeezes out the life-blood of the vine.*

**22.**

*Here in this tavern-haunt I make my lair,*
*Pawning for wine, heart, soul, and all I wear,*
*Without a hope of bliss, or fear of bale,*
*Rapt above water, earth, and fire, and air.*

**23.**

*Quoth fish to duck, "Twill be a sad affair,*
*If this brook leaves its channel dry and bare ";*
*To whom the duck, "When I am dead and roasted*
*The brook may run with wine for aught I care. "*

**24.**

*From doubt to clear assurance is a breath,*
*A breath from infidelity to faith;*
*O precious breath! enjoy it while you may,*
*'Tis all that life can give, and then comes death.*

**25.**

*Ah! wheel of heaven to tyranny inclined,*
*'Twas e'er your wont to show yourself unkind;*
*And, cruel earth, if they should cleave your breast,*
*What store of buried jewels they would find!*

**26.**

*My life lasts but a day or two, and fast*
*Sweeps by, like torrent stream or desert blast,*
*Howbeit, of two days I take no heed—*
*The day to come, and that already past.*

***27.***

*That pearl is from a mine unknown to thee,*
*That ruby bears a stamp thou canst not see,*
*The tale of love some other tongue must tell,*
*All our conjectures are mere fantasy.*

***28.***

*Now with its joyful prime my age is rife,*
*I quaff enchanting wine, and list to fife;*
*Chide not at wine for all its bitter taste,*
*Its bitterness sorts well with human life!*

***29.***

*O soul! whose lot it is to bleed with pain,*
*And daily change of fortune to sustain,*
*Into this body wherefore didst thou come,*
*Seeing thou must at last go forth again?*

***30.***

*To-day is thine to spend, but not to-morrow,*
*Counting on morrows breedeth naught but sorrow;*
*Oh! squander not this breath that heaven hath lent thee,*
*Nor make too sure another breath to borrow!*

***31.***

*'Tis labor lost thus to all doors to crawl,*
*Take thy good fortune, and thy bad withal;*
*Know for a surety each must play his game,*
*As from heaven's dice-box fate's dice chance to fall.*

***32.***

*This jug did once, like me, love's sorrows taste,*

*And bonds of beauty's tresses once embraced,*
*This handle, which you see upon its side,*
*Has many a time twined round a slender waist!*

***33.***

*Days changed to nights, ere you were born, or I,*
*And on its business ever rolled the sky;*
*See you tread gently on this dust-perchance*
*'Twas once the apple of some beauty's eye.*

***34.***

*Pagodas, just as mosques, are homes of prayer,*
*'Tis prayer that church-bells chime unto the air,*
*Yea, Church and Kaaba, Rosary and Cross*
*Are all but divers tongues of world-wide prayer.*

***35.***

*'Twas writ at first, whatever was to be,*
*By pen, unheeding bliss or misery,*
*Yea, writ upon the tablet once for all,*
*To murmur or resist is vanity.*

***36.***

*There is a mystery I know full well,*
*Which to all, good and bad, I can not tell;*
*My words are dark, but I can not unfold*
*The secrets of the station where I dwell.*

***37.***

*No base or light-weight coins pass current here,*
*Of such a broom has swept our dwelling clear;*
*Forth from the tavern comes a sage and cries,*
*"Drink! for ye all must sleep through ages drear."*

***38.***

*With outward seeming we can cheat mankind,*
*But to God's will we can but be resigned;*
*The deepest wiles my cunning e'er devised,*
*To balk resistless fate no way could find.*

***39.***

*Is a friend faithless? spurn him as a foe;*
*Upon trustworthy foes respect bestow;*
*Hold healing poison for an antidote,*
*And baneful sweets for deadly eisel know.*

***40.***

*No heart is there but bleeds when torn from Thee,*
*No sight so clear but craves Thy face to see;*
*And though perchance Thou carest not for them,*
*No soul is there but pines with care for Thee.*

***41.***

*Sobriety doth dry up all delight,*
*And drunkenness doth drown my sense outright;*
*There is a middle state, it is my life—*
*Not altogether drunk, nor sober quite.*

***42.***

*Behold these cups! Can He who deigned to make them,*
*In wanton freak let ruin overtake them,*
*So many shapely feet and hands and heads—*
*What love drives Him to make, what wrath to break them?*

***43.***

*Death's terrors spring from baseless fantasy,*
*Death yields the tree of immortality;*
*Since 'Isa breathed new life into my soul,*
*Eternal death has washed its hands of me!*

***44.***

*Like tulips in the Spring your cups lift up,*
*And, with a tulip-cheeked companion, sup*
*With joy your wine, or e'er this azure wheel*
*With some unlooked-for blast upset your cup.*

***45.***

*Facts will not change to humor man's caprice,*
*So vaunt not human powers, but hold your peace;*
*Here must we stay, weighed down with grief for this.*
*That we were born so late, so soon decease.*

***46.***

*Khayyam! why weep you that your life is bad?*
*What boots it thus to mourn? Rather be glad.*
*He that sins not can make no claim to mercy,*
*Mercy was made for sinners—be not sad.*

***47.***

*All mortal ken is bounded by the veil,*
*To see beyond man's sight is all too frail;*
*Yea! earth's dark bosom is his only home:—*
*Alas! 'twere long to tell the doleful tale.*

***48.***

*This faithless world, my home, I have surveyed,*
*Yea, and with all my wit deep question made,*

*But found no moon with face so bright as thine,*
*No cypress in such stateliness arrayed.*

***49.***

*In synagogue and cloister, mosque and school,*
*Hell's terrors and heaven's lures men's bosoms rule,*
*But they who master Allah's mysteries,*
*Sow not this empty chad their hearts to fool.*

***50.***

*You see the world, but all you see is naught,*
*And all you say, and all you hear is naught,*
*Naught the four quarters of the mighty earth,*
*The secrets treasured in your chamber naught.*

***51.***

*I dreamt a sage said, "Wherefore life consume*
*In sleep? Can sleep make pleasure's roses bloom?*
*For gather not with death's twin-brother sleep,*
*Thou wilt have sleep enough within thy tomb! "*

***52.***

*If the heart knew life's secrets here below,*
*At death 'twould know God's secrets too, I trow;*
*But, if you know naught here, while still yourself,*
*To-morrow, stripped of self, what can you know?*

***53.***

*On that dread day, when wrath shall rend the sky,*
*And darkness dim the bright stars' galaxy,*
*I'll seize the Loved One by His skirt, and cry,*
*"Why hast Thou doomed these guiltless ones to die?"*

**54.**

*To knaves Thy secret we must not confide,*
*To comprehend it is to fools denied,*
*See then to what hard case Thou doomest men,*
*Our hopes from one and all perforce we hide.*

**55.**

*Cupbearer! what though fate's blows here betide us,*
*And a safe resting-place be here denied us,*
*So long as the bright wine-cup stands between us,*
*We have the very Truth at hand to guide us.*

**56.**

*Long time in wine and rose I took delight,*
*But then my business never went aright;*
*Since wine could not accomplish my desire,*
*I have abandoned and forsworn it quite.*

**57.**

*Bring wine! my heart with dancing spirit teems,*
*Wake I fortune's waking is as feeting dreams;*
*Quicksilver-like our days are swift of foot,*
*And youthful fire subsides as torrent streams.*

**58.**

*Love's devotees, not Muslims here you see,*
*Not Solomons, but ants of low degree;*
*Here are but faces wan and tattered rags,*
*No store of Cairene cloth or silk have we.*

**59.**

*My law it is in pleasure's paths to stray,*
*My creed to shun the theologic fray;*

*I wedded Luck, and offered her a dower,*
*She said, "I want none, so thy heart be gay."*

***60.***

*From mosque an outcast, and to church a foe,*
*Allah! of what clay didst thou form me so?*
*Like skeptic monk, or ugly courtesan,*
*No hopes have I above, no joys below.*

***61.***

*Men's lusts, like house-dogs, still the house distress*
*With clamor, barking for mere wantonness;*
*Foxes are they, and sleep the sleep of hares;*
*Crafty as wolves, as tigers pitiless.*

***62.***

*Yon turf, fringing the margent of the stream,*
*As down upon a cherub's lip might seem,*
*Or growth from dust of buried tulip cheeks;*
*Tread not that turf with scorn, or light esteem!*

***63.***

*Hearts with the light of love illumined well,*
*Whether in mosque or synagogue they dwell,*
*Have their names written in the book of love,*
*Unvexed by hopes of heaven or fears of hell.*

***64.***

*One draught of wine outweighs the realm of Tus,*
*Throne of Kobad and crown of Kai Kawus;*
*Sweeter are sighs that lovers heave at morn,*
*Than all the groanings zealot breasts produce.*

***65.***

*Though Muslims for my sins condemn and chide me,*
*Like heathens to my idol I confide me;*
*Yea, when I perish of a drunken bout,*
*I'll call on wine, whatever doom betide me.*

***66.***

*In drinking thus it is not my design*
*To riot, or transgress the law divine,*
*No! to attain unconsciousness of self*
*Is the sole cause I drink me drunk with wine.*

***67.***

*Drunkards are doomed to hell, so men declare,*
*Believe it not, 'tis but a foolish scare;*
*Heaven will be empty as this hand of mine,*
*If none who love good drink find entrance there.*

***68.***

*'Tis wrong, according to the strict Koran,*
*To drink in Rajab, likewise in Sha'ban,*
*God and the Prophet claim those months as theirs,*
*Was Ramadan then made for thirsty man?*

***69.***

*Now Ramadan is come, no wine must flow,*
*Our simple pastimes we must now forego,*
*The wine we have in store we must not drink,*
*Nor on our mistresses one kiss bestow.*

***70.***

*What is the world? A caravanserai,*
*A pied pavilion of night and day;*

*A feast whereat a thousand Jamshids sat,*
*A couch whereon a thousand Bahrams lay.*

**71.**

*Now that your roses bloom with Sowers of bliss,*
*To grasp your goblets be not so remiss;*
*Drink while you may! Time is a treacherous foe,*
*You may not see another day like this.*

**72.**

*Here in this palace, where Bahram held sway,*
*The wild roes drop their young, and tigers stray;*
*And that great hunter king—ah! well-a-day!*
*Now to the hunter death is fallen a prey.*

**73.**

*Down fall the tears from skies enwrapt in gloom,*
*Without this drink, the flowers could never bloom!*
*As now these flowerets yield delight to me,*
*So shall my dust yield flowers—God knows for whom.*

**74.**

*To-day is Friday, as the Muslim says,*
*Drink then from bowls served up in quick relays;*
*Suppose on common days you drink one bowl,*
*To-day drink two, for 'tis the prince of days.*

**75.**

*The very wine a myriad forms sustains,*
*And to take shapes of plants and creatures deigns*
*But deem not that its essence ever dies,*
*Its forms may perish, but its self remains.*

***76.***

*'Tis naught but smoke this people's fire doth bear,*
*For my well-being not a soul doth care;*
*With hands fate makes me lift up in despair,*
*I grasp men's skirts, but find no succor there.*

***77.***

*This bosom friend, on whom you so rely,*
*Seems to clear wisdom's eyes an enemy;*
*Choose not your friends from this rude multitude,*
*Their converse is a plague 'tis best to fly.*

***78.***

*O foolish one! this molded earth is naught;*
*This parti-colored vault of heaven is naught;*
*Our sojourn in this seat of life and death*
*Is but one breath, and what is that but naught?*

***79.***

*Some wine, a Houri (Houris if there be),*
*A green bank by a stream, with minstrelsy;—*
*Toil not to find a better Paradise*
*If other Paradise indeed there be!*

***80.***

*To the wine-house I saw the sage repair,*
*Bearing a wine-cup, and a mat for prayer;*
*I said, "O Shaikh, what does this conduct mean?"*
*Said he, "Go drink! the world is naught but air."*

***81.***

*The Bulbul to the garden winged his way,*
*Viewed lily cups, and roses smiling gay,*

*Cried in ecstatic notes, "O live your life,*
*You never will relive this fleeting day. "*

***82.***

*Thy body is a tent, where harborage*
*The Sultan spirit takes for one brief age;*
*When he departs, comes the tent-pitcher death,*
*Strikes it, and onward moves, another stage.*

***83.***

*Khayyam, who long time stitched the tents of learning,*
*Has fallen into a furnace, and lies burning,*
*Death's shears have cut his thread of life asunder,*
*Fate's brokers sell him off with scorn and spurning.*

***84.***

*In the sweet spring a grassy bank I sought,*
*And thither wine, and a fair Houri brought;*
*And, though the people called me graceless dog,*
*Gave not to Paradise another thought!*

***85.***

*Sweet is rose-ruddy wine in goblets gay,*
*And sweet are lute and harp and roundelay;*
*But for the zealot who ignores the cup,*
*'Tis sweet when he is twenty leagues away!*

***86.***

*Life, void of wine, and minstrels with their lutes,*
*And the soft murmurs of Iraqian futes,*
*Were nothing worth: I scan the world and see:*
*Save pleasure, life yields only bitter fruits.*

*87.*

*Make haste! soon must you quit this life below,*
*And pass the veil, and Allah's secrets know;*
*Make haste to take your pleasure while you may,*
*You wot not whence you come, nor whither go.*

**88.**

*Depart we must! what boots it then to be,*
*To walk in vain desires continually?*
*Nay, but if heaven vouchsafe no place of rest,*
*What power to cease our wanderings have we?*

**89.**

*To chant wine's praises is my daily task,*
*I live encompassed by cup, bowl, and flask;*
*Zealot! if reason be thy guide, then know*
*That guide of me doth ofttimes guidance ask.*

**90.**

*O men of morals! why do ye defame,*
*And thus misjudge me? I am not to blame.*
*Save weakness for the grape, and female charms,*
*What sins of mine can any of ye name?*

**91.**

*Who treads in passion's footsteps here below,*
*A helpless pauper will depart, I trow;*
*Remember who you are, and whence you come.*
*Consider what you do, and whither go.*

**92.**

*Skies like a zone our weary lives enclose,*
*And from our tear-stained eyes a Jihun flows;*

*Hell is a fire enkindled of our griefs;*
*Heaven but a moment's peace, stolen from our woes.*

**93.**

*I drown in sin—show me Thy clemency!*
*My soul is dark—make me Thy light to see!*
*A heaven that must be earned by painful works,*
*I call a wage, not a gift fair and free.*

**94.**

*Did He who made me fashion me for hell,*
*Or destine me for heaven? I can not tell.*
*Yet will I not renounce cup, lute, and love,*
*Nor earthly cash for heavenly credit sell.*

**95.**

*From right and left the censors came and stood,*
*Saying, "Renounce this wine, this foe of good";*
*But if wine be the foe of holy faith,*
*By Allah, right it is to drink its blood!*

**96.**

*The good and evil with man's nature blent,*
*The weal and woe that heaven's decrees have sent—*
*Impute them not to motions of the skies—*
*Skies than thyself ten times more impotent.*

**97.**

*Against death's arrows what are buckles worth?*
*What all the pomps and riches of the earth?*
*When I survey the world, I see no good*
*But goodness, all beside is nothing worth.*

***98.***

*Weak souls, who from the world can not refrain,*
*Hold life-long fellowship with rule and pain;*
*Hearts free from worldly cares have store of bliss,*
*All others seeds of bitter woe contain.*

***99.***

*He, in whose bosom wisdom's seed is sown,*
*To waste a single day was never known;*
*Either he strives to work great Allah's will,*
*Or else exalts the cup, and works his own.*

***100.***

*When Allah mixed my clay He knew full well*
*My future acts, and could each one foretell;*
*Without His will no act of mine was wrought;*
*Is it then just to punish me in hell?*

***101.***

*Ye, who cease not to drink on common days,*
*Do not on Friday quit your drinking ways;*
*Adopt my creed, and count all days the same,*
*Be worshipers of God, and not of days.*

***102.***

*If grace be grace, and Allah gracious be,*
*Adam from Paradise why banished He?*
*Grace to poor sinners shown is grace indeed;*
*In grace hard earned by works no grace I see.*

***103.***

*Dame Fortune's smiles are full of guile, beware!*
*Her scimitar is sharp to smite, take care!*

*If e'er she drop a sweetmeat in thy mouth,*
*'Tis poisonous-to swallow it forbear!*

***104.***

*Where'er you see a rose or tulip bed,*
*Know that a mighty monarch's blood was shed*
*And where the violet rears her purple tuft,*
*Be sure a black-moled girl hath laid her head.*

***105.***

*Wine is a melting ruby, cup its mine;*
*Cup is the body, and the soul is wine;*
*These crystal goblets smile with ruddy wine*
*Like tears, that blood of wounded hearts enshrine.*

***106.***

*Drink wine! 'tis life etern, and travail's meed,*
*Fruitage of youth, and balm of age's need:*
*'Tis the glad time of roses, wine, and friends;*
*Rejoice thy spirit—that is life indeed.*

***107.***

*Drink wine! long must you sleep within the tomb,*
*Without a friend, or wife to cheer your gloom;*
*Hear what I say, and tell it not again,*
*"Never again can withered tulips bloom. "*

***108.***

*They preach how sweet those Houri brides will be,*
*But I say wine is sweeter—taste and see!*
*Hold fast this cash, and let that credit go,*
*And shun the din of empty drums like me.*

***109.***

*Once and again my soul did me implore,*
*To teach her, if I might, the heavenly lore;*
*I bade her learn the* Alif *well by heart.*
*Who knows that letter well need learn no more.*

***110.***

*I came not hither of my own free will,*
*And go against my wish, a puppet still;*
*Cupbearer! gird thy loins, and fetch some wine;*
*To purge the world's despite, my goblet fill.*

***111.***

*How long must I make bricks upon the sea?*
*Beshrew this vain task of idolatry;*
*Call not Khayyam a denizen of hell;*
*One while in heaven, and one in hell is he.*

***112.***

*Sweet is the breath of Spring to rose's face,*
*And thy sweet face adds charm to this fair place;*
*To-day is sweet, but yesterday is sad,*
*And sad all mention of its parted grace.*

***113.***

*To-night pour wine, and sing a dulcet air,*
*And I upon thy lips will hang, O fair;*
*Yea, pour some wine as rosy as thy cheeks,*
*My mind is troubled like thy ruffled hair.*

***114.***

*Pen, tablet, heaven and hell I looked to see*
*Above the skies, from all eternity;*

*At last the master sage instructed me,*
*"Pen, tablet, heaven and hell are all in thee. "*

***115.***

*The fruit of certitude he can not pluck,*
*The path that leads thereto who never struck,*
*Nor ever shook the bough with strenuous hand;*
*To-day is lost; hope for to-morrow's luck.*

***116.***

*Now spring-tide showers its foison on the land,*
*And lively hearts wend forth, a joyous band,*
*For 'Isa's breath wakes the dead earth to life,*
*And trees gleam white with flowers, like Musa's hand.*

***117.***

*Alas for that cold heart, which never glows*
*With love, nor e'er that charming madness knows;*
*The days misspent with no redeeming love;—*
*No days are wasted half as much as those!*

***118.***

*The zephyrs waft thy fragrance, and it takes*
*My heart, and me, his master, he forsakes;*
*Careless of me he pants and leaps to thee,*
*And thee his pattern and ensample makes!*

***119.***

*Drink wine! and then as Mahmud thou wilt reign,*
*And hear a music passing David's strain:*
*Think not of past or future, seize to-day,*
*Then all thy life will not be lived in vain.*

***120.***

*Ten Powers, and nine spheres, eight heavens made He,*

*And planets seven, of six sides, as we see,*

*Five senses, and four elements, three souls,*

*Two worlds, but only one, O man, like thee.*

***121.***

*Jewry hath seen a thousand prophets die,*

*Sinai a thousand Musas mount the sky;*

*How many Caesars Rome's proud forum crossed!*

*'Neath Wasra's dome how many monarchs lie!*

***122.***

*Gold breeds not wit, but to wit lacking bread*

*Earth's flowery carpet seems a dungeon bed;*

*'Tis his full purse that makes the rose to smile,*

*While empty-handed violets hang the head.*

***123.***

*Heaven's wheel has made full many a heart to moan,*

*And many a budding rose to earth has thrown;*

*Plume thee not on thy youth and lusty strength,*

*Full many a bud is blasted ere 'tis blown.*

***124.***

*What lord is fit to rule but "Truth "? Not one.*

*What beings disobey His rule? Not one.*

*All things that are, are such as He decrees;*

*And naught is there beside beneath the sun.*

***125.***

*That azure-colored vault and golden tray*

*Have turned, and will turn yet for many a day;*

*And just so we, impelled by turns of fate—*
*Come here but for a while, then pass away.*

***126.***

*The Master did himself these vessels frame,*
*Why should he cast them out to scorn and shame?*
*If he has made them well, why should he break them?*
*Yea, though he marred them, they are not to blame.*

***127.***

*Kindness to friends and foes 'tis well to show,*
*No kindly heart can prove unkind, I trow:*
*Harshness will alienate a bosom friend,*
*And kindness reconcile a deadly foe.*

***128.***

*To lovers true, what matters dark or fair?*
*Or if the loved one silk or sackcloth wear,*
*Or lie on down or dust, or rise to heaven?*
*Yea, though she sink to hell, he'll seek her there.*

***129.***

*Full many a hill and vale I journeyed o'er;*
*Yea, journeyed through the world's wide quarters four,*
*But never heard of pilgrim who returned;*
*When once they go, they go to come no more.*

***130.***

*Wine-houses flourish through this thirst of mine,*
*Loads of remorse weigh down this back of mine;*
*Yet, if I sinned not, what would mercy do?*
*Mercy depends upon these sins of mine.*

***131.***

*Thy being is the being of Another,*
*Thy passion is the passion of Another.*
*Cover thy head, and think, and thou wilt see*
*Thy hand is but the cover of Another.*

***132.***

*From learning to the cup your bridle turn;*
*All lore of world to come, save Kausar, spurn;*
*Your turban pawn for wine, or keep a shred*
*To bind your brow, and all the remnant burn.*

***133.***

*See! from the world what profit have I gained?*
*What fruitage of my life in hand retained?*
*What use is Jamshid's goblet, once 'tis crushed?*
*What pleasure's torch, when once its light has waned?*

***134.***

*When life is spent, what's Balkh or Nishapore?*
*What sweet or bitter, when the cup runs o'er?*
*Come drink! full many a moon will wax and wane*
*In times to come, when we are here no more.*

***135.***

*O fair! whose cheeks checkmate red eglantine,*
*And draw the game with those fair maids of Chin;*
*You played one glance against the king of Babil*
*And took his pawns, and knights, and rooks, and queen.*

***136.***

*Life's caravan is hastening on its way;*

*Brood not on troubles of the coming day,*
*But fill the wine-cup ere sweet night be gone,*
*And snatch a pleasant moment, while you may.*

***137.***

*He, who the world's foundations erst did lay,*
*Doth bruise full many a bosom day by day,*
*And many a ruby lip and musky tress*
*Doth coffin in the earth, and shroud with clay.*

***138.***

*Be not beguiled by world's insidious wiles;*
*O foolish ones, ye know her tricks and guiles;*
*Your precious lifetime cast not to the winds;*
*Haste to seek wine, and court a sweetheart's smile.*

***139.***

*Comrades! I pray you, physic me with wine,*
*Make this wan amber face like rubies shine,*
*And, if I die, use wine to wash my corpse,*
*And frame my coffin out of planks of vine!*

***140.***

*When Allah yoked the courses of the sun,*
*And launched the Pleiades their race to run,*
*My lot was fixed in fate's high chancery;*
*Then why blame me for wrong that fate has done?*

***141.***

*Ah! seasoned wine oft falls to rawest fools,*
*And clumsiest workmen own the finest tools;*
*And Turki maids, fit to delight men's hearts,*
*Lavish their smiles on beardless boys in school!*

***142.***

*Whilom, ere youth's conceit had waned, methought*
*Answers to all life's problems I had wrought;*
*But now, grown old and wise, too late I see*
*My life is spent, and all my lore is naught.*

***143.***

*They who of prayer-mats make such great display*
*Are fools to bear hypocrisy's hard sway;*
*Strange! under cover of this saintly show*
*They live like heathen, and their faith betray.*

***144.***

*To him who would his sins extenuate,*
*Let pious men this verse reiterate,*
*"To call God's prescience the cause of sin*
*In wisdom's purview is but folly's prate. "*

***145.***

*He brought me hither, and I felt surprise,*
*From life I gather but a dark surmise,*
*I go against my will;—thus, why I come,*
*Why live, why go, are all dark mysteries.*

***146.***

*When I recall my grievous sins to mind,*
*Fire burns my breast, and tears my vision blind;*
*Yet, when a slave repents, is it not meet*
*His lord should pardon, and again be kind?*

***147.***

*They at whose lore the whole world stands amazed,*
*Whose high thoughts, like Borak, to heaven are raised,*

*Strive to know Thee in vain, and like heaven's wheel*
*Their heads are turning, and their brains are dazed.*

**148.**

*Allah hath promised wine in Paradise,*
*Why then should wine on earth be deemed a vice?*
*An Arab in his cups cut Hamzah's girths—*
*For that sole cause was drink declared a vice.*

**149.**

*Now of old joys naught but the name is left,*
*Of all old friends but wine we are bereft,*
*And that wine new, but still cleave to the cup,*
*For save the cup, what single joy is left?*

**150.**

*The world will last long after Khayyam's fame*
*Has passed away, yea, and his very name;*
*Aforetime we were not, and none did heed.*
*When we are dead and gone, 'twill be tie same.*

**151.**

*The sages who have compassed sea and land,*
*Their secret to search out, and understand—*
*My mind misgives me if they ever solve*
*The scheme on which this universe is planned.*

**152.**

*Ah! wealth takes wings, and leaves our hands all bare,*
*And death's rough hands delight our hearts to tear;*
*And from the nether world none e'er escapes,*
*To bring us news of the poor pilgrims there.*

***153.***

*'Tis passing strange, those titled noblemen*
*Find their own lives a burden sore, but when*
*They meet with poorer men, not slaves to sense,*
*They scarcely deign to reckon them as men.*

***154.***

*The wheel on high, still busied with despite,*
*Will ne'er unloose a wretch from his sad plight;*
*But when it lights upon a smitten heart,*
*Straightway essays another blow to smite.*

***155.***

*Now is the volume of my youth outworn,*
*And all my spring-tide blossoms rent and torn.*
*Ah, bird of youth! I marked not when you came*
*Nor when you fled, and left me thus forlorn.*

***156.***

*These fools, by dint of ignorance most crass,*
*Think they in wisdom all mankind surpass;*
*And glibly do they damn as infidel*
*Whoever is not, like themselves, an ass.*

***157.***

*Still be the wine-house thronged with its glad choir,*
*And Pharisaic skirts burnt up with fire;*
*Still be those tattered frocks and azure robes*
*Trod under feet of revelers in the mire.*

***158.***

*Why toil ye to ensure illusions vain,*
*And good or evil of the world attain?*

*Ye rise like Zamzam, or the fount of life,*
*And, like them, in earth's bosom sink again.*

***159.***

*Till the Friend pours his wine to glad my heart,*
*No kisses to my face will heaven impart:*
*They say, "Repent in time "; but how repent,*
*Ere Allah's grace hath softened my hard heart?*

***160.***

*When I am dead, take me and grind me small,*
*So that I be a caution unto all,*
*And knead me into clay with wine, and then*
*Use me to stop the wine-jar's mouth withal.*

***161.***

*What though the sky with its blue canopy*
*Doth close us in so that we can not see,*
*In the etern Cupbearer's wine methinks*
*There float a myriad bubbles like to me.*

***162.***

*Take heart! Long in the weary tomb you'll lie,*
*While stars keep countless watches in the sky,*
*And see your ashes molded into bricks,*
*To build another's house and turrets high.*

***163.***

*Glad hearts, who seek not notoriety,*
*Nor flaunt in gold and silken bravery,*
*Haunt not this ruined earth like gloomy owls,*
*But wing their way, Simurgh-like, to the sky.*

***164.***

*Wine's power is known to wine-bibbers alone,*
*To narrow heads and hearts 'tis never shown;*
*I blame not them who never felt its force,*
*For, till they feel it, how can it be known?*

***165.***

*Needs must the tavern-hunter bathe in wine,*
*For none can make a tarnished name to shine;*
*Go! bring me wine, for none can now restore*
*Its pristine sheen to this soiled veil of mine.*

***166.***

*I wasted life in hope, yet gatherèd not*
*In all my life of happiness one jot;*
*Now my fear is that life may not endure,*
*Till I have taken vengeance on my lot!*

***167.***

*Be very wary in the soul's domain,*
*And on the world's affairs your lips refrain;*
*Be, as it were, sans tongue, sans ear, sans eye,*
*While tongue, and ears, and eyes you still retain.*

***168.***

*Let him rejoice who has a loaf of bread,*
*A little nest wherein to lay his head,*
*Is slave to none, and no man slaves for him—*
*In truth his lot is wondrous well bested.*

***169.***

*What adds my service to Thy majesty?*
*Or how can sin of mine dishonor Thee?*

*O pardon, then, and punish not, I know*
*Thou'rt slow to wrath, and prone to clemency.*

***170.***

*Hands, such as mine, that handle bowls of wine,*
*'Twere shame to book and pulpit to confine;*
*Zealot! thou'rt dry, and I am moist with drink,*
*Yea, far too moist to catch that fire of thine!*

***171.***

*Whoso aspires to gain a rose-cheeked fair,*
*Sharp pricks from fortune's thorns must learn to bear.*
*See! till this comb was cleft by cruel cuts,*
*It never dared to touch my lady's hair.*

***172.***

*Forever may my hands on wine be stayed,*
*And my heart pant for some fair Houri maid!*
*They say, "May Allah aid thee to repent!"*
*Repent I could not, e'en with Allah's aid!*

***173.***

*Soon shall I go, by time and fate deplored,*
*Of all my precious pearls not one is bored;*
*Alas! there die with me a thousand truths*
*To which these fools fit audience ne'er accord.*

***174.***

*To-day how sweetly breathes the temperate air,*
*The rains have newly laved the parched parterre;*
*And Bulbuls cry in notes of ecstasy,*
*"Thou too, O pallid rose, our wine must share! "*

*175.*

*Ere you succumb to shocks of mortal pain,*
*The rosy grape-juice from your wine-cup drain.*
*You are not gold, that, hidden in the earth,*
*Your friends should care to dig you up again!*

*176.*

*My coming brought no profit to the sky,*
*Nor does my going swell its majesty;*
*Coming and going put me to a stand,*
*Ear never heard their wherefore nor their why.*

*177.*

*The heavenly Sage, whose wit exceeds compare,*
*Counteth each vein, and numbereth every hair;*
*Men you may cheat by hypocritic arts,*
*But how cheat Him to whom all hearts are bare?*

*178.*

*Ah! wine lends wings to many a weary wight,*
*And beauty spots to ladies' faces bright;*
*All Ramadan I have not drunk a drop,*
*Thrice welcome, then, O Bairam's blessed night!*

*179.*

*All night in deep bewilderment I fret,*
*With tear-drops big as pearls my breast is wet;*
*I can not fill my cranium with wine;*
*How can it hold wine, when 'tis thus upset?*

*180.*

*To prayer and fasting when my heart inclined,*
*All my desire I surely hoped to find;*

*Alas! my purity is stained with wine,*
*My prayers are wasted like a breath of wind.*

***181.***

*I worship rose-red cheeks with heart and soul,*
*I suffer not my hand to quit the bowl,*
*I make each part of me his function do,*
*Or e'er my parts be swallowed in the Whole.*

***182.***

*This worldly love of yours is counterfeit,*
*And, like a half-spent blaze, lacks light and heat;*
*True love is his, who for days, months, and years,*
*Rests not, nor sleeps, nor craves for drink or meat.*

***183.***

*Why spend life in vainglorious essay*
*All Being and Not-being to survey?*
*Since Death is ever pressing at your heels,*
*'Tis best to drink or dream your life away.*

***184.***

*Some hanker after that vain fantasy*
*Of Houris, feigned in Paradise to be;*
*But, when the veil is lifted, they will find*
*How far they are from Thee, how far from Thee.*

***185.***

*In Paradise, they tell us, Houris dwell,*
*And fountains run with wine and oxymel:*
*If these be lawful in the world to come,*
*Surely 'tis right to love them here as well.*

***186.***

*A draught of wine would make a mountain dance,*
*Base is the churl who looks at wine askance;*
*Wine is a soul our bodies to inspire,*
*A truce to this vain talk of temperance!*

***187.***

*Oft doth my soul her prisoned state bemoan,*
*Eer earth-born co-mate she would fain disown,*
*And quit, did not the stirrup of the law*
*Upbear her foot from dashing on the stone.*

***188.***

*The moon of Ramadan is risen, see!*
*Alas, our wine must henceforth banished be;*
*Well! on Sha'ban's last day I'll drink enough*
*To keep me drunk till Bairam's jubilee.*

***189.***

*From life we draw now wine, now dregs to drink,*
*Now flaunt in silk, and now in tatters shrink;*
*Such changes wisdom holds of slight account*
*To those who stand on death's appalling drink!*

***190.***

*What sage tne eternal tangle e'er unraveled,*
*Or one short step beyond his nature traveled?*
*From pupils to the masters turn your eyes,*
*And see, each mother's son alike is graveled.*

***191.***

*Crave not of worldly sweets to take your fill,*
*Nor wait on turn of fortune, good or ill;*

*Be of light heart, as are the skies above,*
*They roll a round or two, and then lie still.*

***192.***

*What eye can pierce the veil of God's decrees,*
*Or read the riddle of earth's destinies?*
*Pondered have I for years threescore and ten,*
*But still am baffled by these mysteries.*

***193.***

*They say, when the last trump shall sound its knell,*
*Our Friend will sternly judge, and doom to hell.*
*Can aught but good from perfect goodness come?*
*Compose your trembling hearts, 'twill all be well.*

***194.***

*Drink wine to root up metaphysic weeds,*
*And tangle of the two-and-seventy creeds;*
*Do not forswear that wondrous alchemy,*
*'Twill turn to gold, and cure a thousand needs.*

***195.***

*Though drink is wrong, take care with whom you drink,*
*And who you are that drink, and what you drink;*
*And drink at will, for, these three points observed,*
*Who but the very wise can ever drink?*

***196.***

*To drain a gallon beaker I design,*
*Yea, two great beakers, brimmed with richest wine;*
*Old faith and reason thrice will I divorce,*
*Then take to wife the daughter of the vine.*

***197.***

*True I drink wine, like every man of sense,*
*For I know Allah will not take offense;*
*Before time was, He know that I should drink,*
*And who am I to thwart His prescience?*

***198.***

*Rich men, who take to drink, the world defy*
*With shameless riot, and as beggars die;*
*Place in my ruby pipe some emerald hemp,*
*'Twill do as well to blind care's serpent eye.*

***199.***

*These fools have never burnt the midnight oil*
*In deep research, nor do they ever toil*
*To step beyond themselves, but dress them fine,*
*And plot of credit others to despoil.*

***200.***

*When false dawn streaks the east with cold, gray line,*
*Pour in your cups the pure blood of the vine;*
*The truth, they say, tastes bitter in the mouth,*
*This is a token that the "Truth " is wine.*

***201.***

*Now is the time earth decks her greenest bowers,*
*And trees, like Musa's hand, grow white with flowers!*
*As 'twere at 'Isa's breath the plants revive,*
*While clouds brim o'er, like tearful eyes, with showers.*

***202.***

*Oh burden not thyself with drudgery,*

*Lord of white silver and red gold to be;*
*But feast with friends, ere this warm breath of thine*
*Be chilled in death, and earthworms feast on thee.*

***203.***

*The showers of grape juice, which cupbearers pour,*
*Quench fires of grief in many a sad heart's core.*
*Praise be to Allah, who hath sent this balm*
*To heal sore hearts, and spirits' health restore!*

***204.***

*Can alien Pharisees Thy kindness tell,*
*Like us, Thy intimates, who nigh Thee dwell?*
*Thou say'st, "All sinners will I burn with fire."*
*Say that to strangers-we know Thee too well.*

***205.***

*O comrades dear, when hither ye repair*
*In times to come, communion sweet to share,*
*While the cupbearer pours your old Magh wine,*
*Call poor Khayyam to mind, and breathe a prayer.*

***206.***

*For me heaven's sphere no music ever made,*
*Nor yet with soothing voice my fears allayed;*
*If e'er I found brief respite from my woes,*
*Back to woe's thrall I was at once betrayed.*

***207.***

*Sooner with half a loaf contented be,*
*And water from a broken crock, like me,*
*Than lord it over one poor fellow man,*
*Or to another bow the vassal knee.*

***208.***

*While Moon and Venus in the sky shall dwell,*
*None shall see aught red grape-juice to excel:*
*O foolish publicans, what can you buy*
*One half so precious as the goods you sell?*

***209.***

*They who by genius, and by power of brain,*
*The rank of man's enlighteners attain,*
*Not even they emerge from this dark night,*
*But tell their dreams, and fall asleep again.*

***210.***

*At dawn, when dews bedeck the tulip's face,*
*And violets their heavy heads abase,*
*I love to see the roses' folded buds,*
*With petals closed against the wind's disgrace.*

***211.***

*Like as the skies rain down sweet jessamine,*
*And sprinkle all the meads with eglantine,*
*Right so, from out this jug of violet hue,*
*I pour in lily cups this rosy wine.*

***212.***

*Ah! thou hast snared this head, though white as snow,*
*Which oft has vowed the wine-cup to forego;*
*And wrecked the mansion long resolve did build,*
*And rent the vesture penitence did sew!*

***213.***

*I am not one whom Death doth much dismay,*
*Life's terrors all Death's terrors far outweigh;*

*This life, that Heaven hath lent me for a while,*
*I will pay back, when it is time to pay.*

***214.***

*The stars, who dwell on heaven's exalted stage,*
*Baffle the wise diviners of our age;*
*Take heed, hold fast the rope of mother wit.*
*These augurs all distrust their own presage.*

***215.***

*The people who the heavenly world adorn,*
*Who come each night, and go away each morn,*
*Now on Heaven's skirt, and now in earth's deep pouch,*
*While Allah lives, shall aye anew be born!*

***216.***

*Slaves of vain wisdom and philosophy,*
*Who toil at Being and Nonentity,*
*Parching your brains till they are like dry grapes,*
*Be wise in time, and drink grapejuice like me!*

***217.***

*Sense, seeking happiness, bids us pursue*
*All present joys, and present griefs eschew;*
*She says, we are not as the meadow grass,*
*Which, when they mow it down, springs up anew.*

***218.***

*Now Ramadan is past, Shawwal comes back,*
*And feast and song and joy no more we lack;*
*The wine-skin carriers throng the streets and cry,*
*"Here comes the porter with his precious pack. "*

**219.**

*My comrades are all gone; Death, deadly foe,*
*Has caught them one by one, and trampled low;*
*They shared life's feast, and drank its wine with me,*
*But lost their heads, and dropped a while ago.*

**220.**

*Those hypocrites, all know so well, who lurk*
*In streets to beg their bread, and will not work,*
*Claim to be saints, like Shibli and Junaid,*
*No Shiblis are they, though well known in Karkh!*

**221.**

*When the great Founder molded me of old,*
*He mixed much baser metal with my gold;*
*Better or fairer I can never be*
*Than I first issued from his heavenly mold.*

**222.**

*The joyous souls who quaff potations deep,*
*And saints who in the mosques sad vigils keep,*
*Are lost at sea alike, and find no shore,*
*One only wakes, all others are asleep.*

**223.**

*Not-being's water served to mix my clay,*
*And on my heart grief's fire doth ever prey,*
*And blown am I like wind about the world,*
*And last my crumbling earth is swept away.*

**224.**

*Small gains to learning on this earth accrue,*
*They pluck life's fruitage, learning who eschew;*

*Take pattern by the fools who learning shun,*
*And then perchance shall fortune smile on you.*

***225.***

*When the fair soul this mansion doth vacate,*
*Each element assumes its primal state,*
*And all the silken furniture of life*
*Is then dismantled by the blows of fate.*

***226.***

*These people string their beads of learned lumber,*
*And tell of Allah stories without number;*
*Yet never solve the riddle of the skies,*
*But wag the chin, and get them back to slumber.*

***227.***

*These folk are asses, laden with conceit,*
*And glittering drums, that empty sounds repeat,*
*And humble slaves are they of name and fame,*
*Acquire a name, and, lo! they kiss thy feet.*

***228.***

*On the dread day of final scrutiny*
*Thou wilt be rated by thy quality;*
*Get wisdom ana fair qualities to-day,*
*For, as thou art, requited wilt thou be.*

***229.***

*Many fine heads, like bowls, the Brazier made,*
*And thus his own similitude portrayed;*
*He sets one upside down above our heads,*
*Which keeps us all continually afraid.*

***230.***

*My true condition I may thus explain*
*In two short verses which the whole contain:*
*"From love to Thee I now lay down my life,*
*In hope Thy love will raise me up again.*

***231.***

*The heart, like tapers, takes at beauty's eyes*
*A flame, and lives by that whereby it dies;*
*And beauty is a flame where hearts, like moths,*
*Offer themselves a burning sacrifice.*

***232.***

*To please the righteous life itself I sell,*
*And, though they tread me down, never rebel;*
*Men say, "Inform us what and where is hell?"*
*Ill company will make this earth a hell.*

***233.***

*The sun doth smite the roofs with Orient ray*
*And, Khosrau like, his wine-red sheen display;*
*Arise, and drink! the herald of the dawn*
*Uplifts his voice, and cries, "Oh, drink to-day!"*

***234.***

*Comrades! when e'er you meet together here,*
*Recall your friend to mind, and drop a tear;*
*And when the circling wine-cups reach his seat,*
*Pray turn one upside down his dust to cheer.*

***235.***

*That grace and favor at the first, what meant it?*
*That lavishing of joy and peace, what meant it?*

*But now thy purpose is to grieve my heart;*
*What did I do to cause this change? What meant it?*

***236.***

*These hypocrites who build on saintly show,*
*Treating the body as the spirit's foe,*
*If they will shut their mouths with lime, like jars,*
*My jar of grape-juice I will then forego.*

***237.***

*Many have come, and run their eager race,*
*Striving for pleasures, luxuries, or place,*
*And quaffed their wine, and now all silent lie,*
*Enfolded in their parent earth's embrace.*

***238.***

*Then, when the good reap fruits of labors past,*
*My hapless lot with drunkards will be cast;*
*If good, may I be numbered with the first,*
*If bad, find grace and mercy with the last.*

***239.***

*Of happy turns of fortune take your fill,*
*Seek pleasure's couch, or wine-cup, as you will;*
*Allah regards not if you sin, or saint it,*
*So take your pleasure, be it good or ill.*

***240.***

*Heaven multiplies our sorrows day by day,*
*And grants no joys it does not take away;*
*If those unborn could know the ills we bear,*
*What think you, would they rather come or stay?*

***241.***

*Why ponder thus the future to foresee,*
*And jade thy brain to vain perplexity?*
*Cast off thy care, leave Allah's plans to him—*
*He formed them all without consulting thee.*

***242.***

*The tenants of the tombs to dust decay,*
*Nescient of self, and all beside are they;*
*Their sundered atoms float about the world,*
*Like mirage clouds, until the judgment-day.*

***243.***

*O soul! lay up all earthly goods in store,*
*Thy mead with pleasure's flowerets spangled o'er;*
*And know 'tis all as dew, that decks the flowers*
*For one short night, and then is seen no more!*

***244.***

*Heed not the Sunna, nor the law divine;*
*If to the poor his portion you assign,*
*And never injure one, nor yet abuse,*
*I guarantee you heaven, and now some wine!*

***245.***

*Vexed by this wheel of things, that pets the base,*
*My sorrow-laden life drags on apace;*
*Like rosebud, from the storm I wrap me close,*
*And blood-spots on my heart, like tulip, trace.*

***246.***

*Youth is the time to pay court to the vine,*
*To quaff the cup, with revelers to recline;*

*A flood of water once laid waste the earth,*
*Hence learn to lay you waste with floods of wine.*

**247.**

*The world is baffled in its search for Thee,*
*Wealth can not find Thee, no, nor poverty;*
*Thou'rt very near us, but our ears are deaf,*
*Our eyes are blinded that we may not see!*

**248.**

*Take care you never hold a drinking-bout*
*With an ill-tempered, ill-conditioned lout;*
*He'll make a vile disturbance all night long,*
*And vile apologies next day, no doubt.*

**249.**

*The starry aspects are not all benign;*
*Why toil then after vain desires, and pine*
*To lade thyself with load of fortune's boons,*
*Only to drop it with this life of thine?*

**250.**

*O comrades! here is filtered wine, come drink!*
*Pledge all your charming sweethearts as you drink;*
*'Tis the grape's blood, and this is what it says,*
*"To you I dedicate my life-blood! drink! "*

**251.**

*Are you depressed? Then take of bhang one grain,*
*Of rosy grape-juice take one pint or twain;*
*Sufis, you say, must not take this or that,*
*Then go and eat the pebbles off the plain!*

**252.**

*I saw a busy potter by the way*
*Kneading with might and main a lump of clay;*
*And, lo! the clay cried, "Use me gently, pray;*
*I was a man myself but yesterday!"*

**253.**

*Oh! wine is richer that the realm of Jam,*
*More fragrant than the food of Miriam;*
*Sweeter are sighs that drunkards heave at morn*
*Than strains of Bu Sa'id and Bin Adham.*

**254.**

*Deep in the rondure of the heavenly blue,*
*There is a cup, concealed from mortals' view,*
*Which all must drink in turn; Oh, sigh not then,*
*But drink it boldly, when it comes to you!*

**255.**

*Though you should live to four, or forty score,*
*Go hence you must, as all have gone before;*
*Then, be you king, or beggar of the streets,*
*They'll rate you all the same, no less, no more.*

**256.**

*If you seek Him, abandon child and wife,*
*Arise, and sever all these ties to life;*
*All these are bonds to check you on your course.*
*Arise, and cut these bonds, as with a knife.*

**257.**

*O heart! this world is but a fleeting show,*
*Why should its empty griefs distress thee so?*

*Bow down, and bear thy fate, the eternal pen*
*Will not unwrite its roll for thee, I trow!*

**258.**

*Whoe'er returned of all that went before,*
*To tell of that long road they travel o'er?*
*Leave naught undone of what you have to do,*
*For when you go, you will return no more.*

**259.**

*Dark wheel! how many lovers thou hast slain,*
*Like Mahmud and Ayaz, O inhumane!*
*Come, let us drink, thou grantest not two lives;*
*When one is spent, we find it not again.*

**260.**

*Illustrious Prophet! whom all kings obey,*
*When is our darkness lightened by wine's ray?*
*On Sunday, Monday, Tuesday, Wednesday, Thursday,*
*Friday, and Saturday, both night and day!*

**261.**

*O turn away those roguish eyes of thine!*
*Be still! seek not my peace to undermine!*
*Thou say'st, "Look not. " I might as well essay*
*To slant my goblet, and not spill my wine.*

**262.**

*In taverns better far commune with Thee,*
*Than pray in mosques, and fail Thy face to see!*
*O first and last of all Thy creatures Thou,*
*'Tis Thine to burn, and Thine to cherish me!*

***263.***

*To wise and worthy men your life devote,*
*But from the worthless keep your walk remote;*
*Dare to take poison from a sage's hand,*
*But from a fool refuse an antidote.*

***264.***

*I flew here, as a bird from the wild, in aim*
*Up to a higher nest my course to frame;*
*But, finding here no guide who knows the way,*
*Fly out by the same door where through I came.*

***265.***

*He binds us in resistless Nature's chain,*
*And yet bids us our natures to restrain;*
*Between these counter rules we stand perplexed,*
*"Hold the jar slant, but all the wine retain.*

***266.***

*They go away, and none is seen returning,*
*To teach that other world's recondite learning;*
*'Twill not be shown for dull mechanic prayers,*
*For prayer is naught without true heartfelt yearning.*

***267.***

*Go to! Cast dust on those deaf skies, who spurn*
*Thy orisons and bootless prayers, and learn*
*To quaff the cup, and hover round the fair;*
*Of all who go, did ever one return?*

***268.***

*Though Khayyam strings no pearls of righteous deeds,*
*Nor sweeps from off his soul sin's noisome weeds,*

*Yet will he not despair of heavenly grace,*
*Seeing that One as two he ne'er misreads.*

**269.**

*Again to tavern-haunts do we repair,*
*And say "Adieu " to the five hours of prayer;*
*Where'er we see a long-necked flask of wine,*
*We elongate our necks that wine to share.*

**270.**

*We are but chessmen, destined, it is plain,*
*That great chess-player, Heaven, to entertain;*
*It moves us on life's chess-board to and fro,*
*And then in death's dark box shuts up again.*

**271.**

*You ask what is this life so frail, so vain,*
*'Tis long to tell, yet will I make it plain;*
*'Tis but a breath blown from the vasty deeps,*
*And then blown back to those same deeps again!*

**272.**

*To-day to heights of rapture have I soared,*
*Yea, and with drunken Maghs pure wine adored;*
*I am become beside myself, and rest*
*In that pure temple, "Am not I your Lord?"*

**273.**

*My queen (long may she live to vex her slave!)*
*To-day a token of affection gave,*
*Darting a kind glance from her eyes, she passed,*
*And said, "Do good and cast it on the wave!"*

***274.***

*I put my lips to the cup, for I did yearn*
*The hidden cause of length of days to learn;*
*He leaned his lip to mine, and whispered low,*
*"Drink! for, once gone, you never will return. "*

***275.***

*We lay in the cloak of Naught, asleep and still,*
*Thou said'st, "Awake! taste the world's good and ill";*
*Here we are puzzled by Thy strange command,*
*From slanted jars no single drop to spill.*

***276.***

*O Thou! who know'st the secret thoughts of all,*
*In time of sorest need who aidest all,*
*Grant me repentance, and accept my plea,*
*O Thou who dost accept the pleas of all!*

***277.***

*I saw a bird perched on the walls of Tus,*
*Before him lay the skull of Kai Kawus,*
*And thus he made his moan, "Alas, poor king!*
*Thy drums are hushed, thy 'larums have rung truce. "*

***278.***

*Ask not the chances of the time to be,*
*And for the past, 'tis vanished, as you see;*
*This ready-money breath set down as gain,*
*Future and past concern not you or me.*

***279.***

*What launched that golden orb his course to run,*

*What wrecks his firm foundations, when 'tis done,*
*No man of science ever weighed with scales,*
*Nor made assay with touchstone, no, not one!*

***280.***

*I pray thee to my counsel lend thine ear,*
*Cast off this false hypocrisy's veneer;*
*This life a moment is, the next all time;*
*Sell not eternity for earthly gear!*

***281.***

*Ofttimes I plead my foolishness to Thee,*
*My heart contracted with perplexity;*
*I gird me with the Magian zone, and why?*
*For shame so poor a Mussulman to be.*

***282.***

*Khayyam! rejoice that wine you still can pour,*
*And still the charms of tulip cheeks adore;*
*You'll soon not be, rejoice then that you are,*
*Think how 'twould be in case you were no more!*

***283.***

*Once, in a potter's shop, a company*
*Of cups in converse did I chance to see,*
*And lo! one lifted up his voice, and cried,*
*"Who made, who sells, who buys this crockery? "*

***284.***

*Last night, as I reeled from the tavern door,*
*I saw a sage, who a great wine-jug bore;*
*I said, "O Shaikh, have you no shame?" Said he,*
*"Allah hath boundless mercy in his store. "*

***285.***

*Life's fount is wine, Khizir its guardian,*
*I, like Elias, find it where I can;*
*'Tis sustenance for heart and spirit too,*
*Allah himself calls wine "a boon to man."*

***286.***

*Though wine is banned, yet drink, forever drink!*
*By day and night, with strains of music drink!*
*Where'er thou lightest on a cup of wine,*
*Spill just one drop, and take the rest and drink!*

***287.***

*Although the creeds number some seventy-three,*
*I hold with none but that of loving Thee;*
*What matter faith, unfaith, obedience, sin?*
*Thou'rt all we need, the rest is vanity.*

***288.***

*Tell one by one my scanty virtues o'er;*
*As for my sins, forgive them by the score;*
*Let not my faults kindle Thy wrath to flame;*
*By blest Mohammed's tomb, forgive once more!*

***289.***

*Grieve not at coming ill, you can't defeat it,*
*And what far-sighted person goes to meet it?*
*Cheer up! bear not about a world of grief,*
*Your fate is fixed, and grieving will not cheat it.*

***290.***

*There is a chalice made with wit profound,*
*With tokens of the Maker's favor crowned;*

*Yet the world's Potter takes his masterpiece,*
*And dashes it to pieces on the ground!*

***291.***

*In truth wine is a spirit thin as air,*
*A limpid soul in the cup's earthen ware;*
*No dull, dense person shall be friend of mine*
*Save wine-cups, which are dense and also rare.*

***292.***

*O wheel of heaven! no ties of bread you feel,*
*No ties of salt, you flay me like an eel!*
*A woman's wheel spins clothes for man and wife,*
*It does more good than you, O heavenly wheel!*

***293.***

*Did no fair rose my paradise adorn,*
*I would make shift to deck it with a thorn;*
*And if I lacked my prayer-mats, beads, and Shaikh,*
*Those Christian bells and stoles I would not scorn.*

***294.***

*"If heaven deny me peace and fame, " I said,*
*"Let it be open war and shame instead;*
*The man who scorns bright wine had best beware,*
*I'll arm me with a stone, and break his head! "*

***295.***

*See! the dawn breaks, and rends night's canopy:*
*Arise! and drain a morning draught with me!*
*Away with gloom! full many a dawn will break*
*Looking for us, and we not here to see!*

***296.***

*O you who tremble not at fires of hell,*
*Nor wash in water of remorse's well,*
*When winds of death shall quench your vital torch,*
*Beware lest earth your guilty dust expel.*

***297.***

*This world a hollow pageant you should deem;*
*All wise men know things are not what they seem;*
*Be of good cheer, and drink, and so shake off*
*This vain illusion of a baseless dream.*

***298.***

*With maids stately as cypresses, and fair*
*As roses newly plucked, your wine-cups share,*
*Or e'er Death's blasts shall rend your robe of fiesh*
*Like yonder rose-leaves, lying scattered there!*

***299.***

*Cast off dull care, O melancholy brother!*
*Woo the sweet daughter of the grape, no other;*
*The daughter is forbidden, it is true,*
*But she is nicer than her lawful mother!*

***300.***

*My love shone forth, and I was overcome,*
*My heart was speaking, but my tongue was dumb;*
*Beside the water-brooks I died of thirst.*
*Was ever known so strange a martyrdom?*

***301.***

*Give me my cup in hand, and sing a glee*
*In concert with the bulbul's symphony;*

*Wine would not gurgle as it leaves the flask,*
*If drinking mute were right for thee and me!*

**302.**

*The "Truth " will not be shown to lofty thought,*
*Nor yet with lavished gold may it be bought;*
*But, if you yield your life for fifty years,*
*From words to "states " you may perchance be brought.*

**303.**

*I solved all problems, down from Saturn's wreath*
*Unto this lowly sphere of earth beneath,*
*And leapt out free from bonds of fraud and lies,*
*Yea, every knot was loosed, save that of death!*

**304.**

*Peace! the eternal "Has been" and "To be"*
*Pass man's experience, and man's theory;*
*In joyful seasons naught can vie with wine,*
*To all these riddles wine supplies the key!*

**305.**

*Allah, our Lord, is merciful, though just;*
*Sinner! despair not, but His mercy trust!*
*For though to-day you perish in your sins,*
*To-morrow He'll absolve your crumbling dust.*

**306.**

*Your course annoys me, O ye wheeling skies!*
*Unloose me from your chain of tyrannies!*
*If none but fools your favors may enjoy,*
*Then favor me—I am not very wise!*

***307.***

*O City Mufti, you go more astray*
*Than I do, though to wine I do give way;*
*I drink the blood of grapes, you that of men:*
*Which of us is the more bloodthirsty, pray?*

***308.***

*'Tis well to drink, and leave anxiety*
*For what is past, and what is yet to be;*
*Our prisoned spirits, lent us for a day,*
*A while from season's bondage shall go free!*

***309.***

*When Khayyam quittance at Death's hand receives,*
*And sheds his outworn life, as trees their leaves,*
*Full gladly will he sift this world away,*
*'Ere dustmen sift his ashes in their sieves.*

***310.***

*This wheel of heaven, which makes us all afraid,*
*I liken to a lamp's revolving shade,*
*The sun the candlestick, the earth the shade,*
*And men the trembling forms thereon portrayed.*

***311.***

*Who was it that did mix my clay? Not I.*
*Who spun my web of silk and wool? Not I.*
*Who wrote upon my forehead all my good,*
*And all my evil deeds? In truth not I.*

***312.***

*O let us not forecast to-morrow's fears,*
*But count to-day as gain, my brave compeers!*

*To-morrow we shall quit this inn, and march*
*With comrades who have marched seven thousand years.*

***313.***

*Ne'er for one moment leave your cup unused!*
*Wine keeps heart, faith, and reason too, amused;*
*Had Iblis swallowed but a single drop,*
*To worship Adam he had ne'er refused!*

***314.***

*Come, dance! while we applaud thee, and adore*
*Thy sweet Narcissus eyes, and grape-juice pour;*
*A score of cups is no such great affair,*
*But 'tis enchanting when we reach three score!*

***315.***

*I close the door of hope in my own face,*
*Nor sue for favors from good men, or base;*
*I have but One to lend a helping hand—*
*He knows, as well as I, my sorry case.*

***316.***

*Ah! by these heavens, that ever circling run,*
*And by my own base lusts I am undone,*
*Without the wit to abandon worldly hopes,*
*And wanting sense the world's allures to shun!*

***317.***

*On earth's green carpet many sleepers lie,*
*And hid beneath it others I descry;*
*And others, not yet come, or passed away,*
*People the desert of Non-entity!*

***318.***

*Sure of Thy grace, for sins why need I fear?*
*How can the pilgrim faint whilst Thou art near?*
*On the last day Thy grace will wash me white,*
*And make my "black record " to disappear.*

***319.***

*Think not I dread from out the world to hie,*
*And see my disembodied spirit fly;*
*I tremble not at death, for death is true,*
*'Tis my ill life that makes me fear to die!*

***320.***

*Let us shake off dull reason's incubus,*
*Our tale of days or years cease to discuss,*
*And take our jugs, and plenish them with wine,*
*Or e'er grim potters make their jugs of us!*

***321.***

*How much more wilt thou chide, O raw divine,*
*For that I drink, and am a libertine?*
*Thou hast thy weary beads, and saintly show,*
*Leave me my cheerful sweetheart, and my wine!*

***322.***

*Against my lusts I ever war, in vain,*
*I think on my ill deeds with shame and pain;*
*I trust Thou wilt assoil me of my sins,*
*But even so, my shame must still remain.*

***323.***

*In these twin compasses, O Love, you see*
*One body with two heads, like you and me,*

*Which wander round one center, circlewise,*
*But at the last in one same point agree.*

**324.**

*We shall not stay here long, but while we do,*
*'Tis folly wine and sweethearts to eschew;*
*Why ask if earth etern or transient be?*
*Since you must go, it matters not to you.*

**325.**

*In reverent sort to mosque I wend my way,*
*But, by great Allah, it is not to pray;*
*No! but to steal a prayer-mat! When 'tis worn,*
*I go again, another to purvey.*

**326.**

*No more let fate's annoys our peace consume,*
*But let us rather rosy wine consume;*
*The world our murderer is, and wine its blood,*
*Shall we not then that murderer's blood consume?*

**327.**

*For Thee I vow to cast repute away,*
*And, if I shrink, the penalty to pay;*
*Though life might satisfy Thy cruelty,*
*'Twere naught, I'll bear it till the judgment-day!*

**328.**

*In Being's rondure de we stray belated,*
*Our pride of manhood humbled and abated;*
*Would we were gone! long since have we been wea-*
*ried*
*With this world's griefs, and with its pleasures sated.*

***329.***

*The world is false, so I'll be false as well,*
*And with bright wine, and gladness ever dwell!*
*They say, "May Allah grant thee penitence!"*
*He grants it not, and, did he, I'd rebel!*

***330.***

*When Death shall tread me down upon the plain,*
*And pluck my feathers, and my life-blood drain,*
*Then mold me to a cup, and fill with wine;*
*Haply its scent will make me breathe again.*

***331.***

*So far as this world's dealings I have traced,*
*I find its favors shamefully misplaced;*
*Allah be praised! I see myself debarred*
*From all its boons, and wrongfully disgraced.*

***332.***

*'Tis dawn! my heart with wine I will recruit,*
*And dash to bits the glass of good repute;*
*My long-extending hopes I will renounce,*
*And grasp long tresses, and the charming lute.*

***333.***

*Though I had sinned the sins of all mankind,*
*I know Thou would'st to mercy be inclined;*
*Thou sayest, "I will help in time of need."*
*One needier than I where wilt Thou find?*

***334.***

*Am I a wine-bibber? What if I am?*
*Gueber or infidel? Suppose I am?*

*Each sect miscalls me, but I heed them not,*
*I am my own, and, what I am, I am.*

***335.***

*All my life long from drink I have not ceased.*
*And drink I will to-night on Sadr's feast:*
*And throw my arms about the wine-jar's neck,*
*And kiss its lip, and clasp it to my breast!*

***336.***

*I know what is, and what is not, I know*
*The lore of things above, and things below;*
*But all this lore will cheerfully renounce,*
*If one a higher grade than drink can show.*

***337.***

*Though I drink wine, I am no libertine,*
*Nor am I grasping, save of cups of wine;*
*I scruple to adore myself, like you;*
*For this cause to wine-worship I incline.*

***338.***

*To confidants like you I dare to say*
*What mankind really are—molded of clay,*
*Affliction's clay, and kneaded in distress,*
*They taste the world awhile, then pass away.*

***339.***

*We make the wine-jar's lip our place of prayer,*
*And drink in lessons of true manhood there,*
*And pass our lives in taverns, if perchance*
*The time misspent in mosques we may repair.*

*340.*

*Man is the whole creation's summary,*
*The precious apple of great wisdom's eye;*
*The circle of existence is a ring,*
*Whereof the signet is humanity.*

*341.*

*With fancies, as with wine, our heads we turn,*
*Aspire to heaven, and earth's low trammels spurn;*
*But, when we drop this fleshly clog, 'tis seen*
*From dust we came, and back to dust return.*

*342.*

*If so it be that I did break the fast,*
*Think not I meant it; no! I thought 'twas past—*
*That day more weary than a sleepless night—*
*And blessed breakfast-time had come at last!*

*343.*

*I never drank of joy's sweet cordial,*
*But grief's fell hand infused a drop of gall;*
*Nor dipped my bread in pleasure's piquant salt,*
*But briny sorrow made me smart withal!*

*344.*

*At dawn to tavern-haunts I wend my way,*
*And with distraught Salendars pass the day;*
*O Thou! who know'st things secret, and things known,*
*Grant me Thy grace, that I may learn to pray!*

*345.*

*The world's annoys I rate not at one grain,*
*So I eat once a day I don't complain;*

*And, since earth's kitchen yields no solid food,*
*I pester no man with petitions vain.*

***346.***

*Never from worldly toils have I been free,*
*Never for one short moment glad to be!*
*I served a long apprenticeship to fate,*
*But yet of fortune gained no mastery.*

***347.***

*One hand with Koran, one with wine-cup dight,*
*I half incline to wrong, and half to right;*
*The azure-marbled sky looks down on me,*
*A sorry Muslim, yet not heathen quite.*

***348.***

*Khayyam's respects to Mustafa convey,*
*And with due reverence ask him to say,*
*Why it has pleased him to forbid pure wme,*
*When he allows his people acid whey?*

***349.***

*Tell Khayyam, for a master of the schools,*
*He strangely misinterprets my plain rules:*
*Where have I said that wine is wrong for all?*
*'Tis lawful for the wise, but not for fools.*

***350.***

*My critics call me a philosopher,*
*But Allah knows full well they greatly err;*
*I know not even what I am, much less*
*Why on this earth I am a sojourner!*

***351.***

*The more I die to self, I live the more,*
*The more abase myself, the higher soar;*
*And, strange! the more I drink of Being's wine,*
*More sane I grow and sober than before.*

***352.***

*Quoth rose, "I am the Yusuf flower, I swear,*
*For in my mouth rich golden gems I bear ":*
*I said, "Show me another proof." Quoth she,*
*"Behold this blood-stained vesture that I wear! "*

***353.***

*I studied with the masters long ago,*
*And long ago did master all they know;*
*Here now the end and issue of it all,*
*From earth I came, and like the wind I go!*

***354.***

*Death finds us soiled, though we were pure at birth,*
*With grief we go, although we came with mirth;*
*Watered with tears, and burned with fires of woe,*
*And, casting life to winds, we rest in earth!*

***355.***

*To find great Jamshid's world-reflecting bowl*
*I compassed sea and land, and viewed the whole;*
*But, when I asked the wary sage, I learned*
*That bowl was my own body, and my soul!*

***356.***

*Me, cruel Queen! you love to captivate,*
*And from a knight to a poor pawn trarlslate;*

*You marshal all your force to tire me out,*
*You take my rooks with yours, and then checkmate!*

***357.***

*If Allah wills me not to will aright,*
*Row can I frame my will to will aright?*
*Each single act I will must needs be wrong,*
*Since none but He has power to will aright.*

***358.***

*"For once, while roses are in bloom, " I said,*
*"I'll break the law, and please myself instead,*
*With blooming youths, and maidens' tulip cheeks*
*The plain shall blossom like a tulip-bed. "*

***359.***

*Think not I am existent of myself,*
*Or walk this blood-stained pathway of myself;*
*This being is not I, it is of Him.*
*Pray what, and where, and whence is this "myself"?*

***360.***

*Endure this world without my wine I cannot!*
*Drag on life's load without my cups I cannot!*
*I am the slave of that sweet moment, when*
*They say, "Take one more goblet," and I can not!*

***361.***

*You, who both day and night the world pursue,*
*And thoughts of that dread day of doom eschew,*
*Bethink you of your latter end; be sure*
*As time has treated others, so 'twill you!*

***362.***

*O man, who are creation's summary,*
*Getting and spending too much trouble thee!*
*Arise, and quaff the Etern Cupbearer's wine,*
*And so from troubles of both worlds be free!*

***363.***

*In this eternally revolving zone,*
*Two lucky species of men are known;*
*One knows all good and ill that are on earth,*
*One neither earth's affairs, nor yet his own.*

***364.***

*Make light to me the world's oppressive weight,*
*And hide my failings from the people's hate,*
*And grant me peace to-day, and on the morrow*
*Deal with me as Thy mercy may dictate!*

***365.***

*Souls that are well informed of this world's state,*
*Its weal and woe with equal mind await:*
*For, be it weal we meet, or be it woe,*
*The weal doth pass, and woe too hath its date.*

***366.***

*Lament not fortune's want of constancy,*
*But up! and seize her favors ere they fee;*
*If fortune always cleaved to other men,*
*How could a turn of luck have come to thee?*

***367.***

*Chief of old friends! harken to what I say,*
*Let not heaven's treacherous wheel your heart dis-*

*may;*
*But rest contented in your humble nook,*
*And watch the games that wheel is wont to play.*

**368.**

*Hear now Khayyam's advice, and bear in mind,*
*Consort with revelers, though they be maligned,*
*Cast down the gates of abstinence and prayer,*
*Yea, drink, and even rob, but, oh! be kind!*

**369.**

*This world a body is, and God its soul,*
*And angels are its senses, who control*
*Its limbs—the creatures, elements, and spheres;*
*The One is the sole basis of the whole.*

**370.**

*Last night that idol who enchants my heart,*
*With true desire to elevate my heart,*
*Gave me his cup to drink; when I refused,*
*He said, "Oh, drink to gratify my heart!"*

**371.**

*Would'st thou have fortune bow her neck to thee,*
*Make it thy care to feed thy soul with glee;*
*And hold a creed like mine, which is to drain*
*The cup of wine, not that of misery.*

**372.**

*Though you survey, O my enlightened friend,*
*This world of vanity from end to end,*
*You will discover there no other good*
*Than wine and rosy cheeks, you may depend!*

***373.***

*Last night upon the river bank we lay,*
*I with my wine-cup, and a maiden gay,*
*So bright it shone, like pearl within its shell,*
*The watchman cried, "Behold the break of day!"*

***374.***

*Have you no shame for all the sins you do,*
*Sins of omission and commission, too?*
*Suppose you gain the world, you can but leave it,*
*You can not carry it away with you!*

***375.***

*In a lone waste I saw a debauchee,*
*He had no home, no faith, no heresy,*
*No God, no truth, no law, no certitude;*
*Where in this world is man so bold as he?*

***376.***

*Some look for truth in creeds, and forms, and rules;*
*Some grope for doubts or dogmas in the schools;*
*But from behind the veil a voice proclaims,*
*"Your road lies neither here nor there, O fools. "*

***377.***

*In heaven is seen the bull we name Parwin,*
*Beneath the earth another lurks unseen;*
*And thus to wisdom's eyes mankind appear*
*A drove of asses, two great bulls between!*

***378.***

*The people say, "Why not drink somewhat less?*
*What reasons have you for such great excess? "*

*First, my Love's face, second, my morning draught;*
*Can there be clearer reasons, now confess?*

***379.***

*Had I the power great Allah to advise,*
*I'd bid him sweep away this earth and skies,*
*And build a better, where, unclogged and free,*
*The clear soul might achieve her high emprise.*

***380.***

*This silly sorrow-laden heart of mine*
*Is ever pining for that love of mine;*
*When the Cupbearer poured the wine of love,*
*With my heart's blood he filled this cup of mine!*

***381.***

*To drain the cup, to hover round the fair,*
*Can hypocritic arts with these compare?*
*If all who love and drink are going wrong,*
*There's many a wight of heaven may well despair!*

***382.***

*'Tis wrong with gloomy thoughts your mirth to drown—*
*To let grief's millstone weigh your spirits down;*
*Since none can tell what is to be, 'tis best*
*With wine and love your heart's desires to crown.*

***383.***

*'Tis well in reputation to abide,*
*'Tis shameful against heaven to rail and chide;*
*Still, head had better ache with over-drink,*
*Than be puffed up with Pharisaic pride!*

***384.***

*O Lord! pity this prisoned heart, I pray,*
*Pity this bosom stricken with dismay!*
*Pardon these hands that ever grasp the cup,*
*These feet that to the tavern ever stray!*

***385.***

*O Lord! from self-conceit deliver me,*
*Sever from self, and occupy with Thee!*
*This self is captive to earth's good and ill,*
*Make me beside myself, and set me free!*

***386.***

*Behold the tricks this wheeling dome doth play,*
*And earth laid bare of old friends torn away!*
*O live this present moment, which is thine,*
*Seek not a morrow, mourn not yesterday!*

***387.***

*Since all man's business in this world of woe*
*Is sorrow's pangs to feel, and grief to know,*
*Happy are they that never come at all,*
*And they that, having come, the soonest go!*

***388.***

*By reason's dictates it is right to live,*
*But of ourselves we know not how to live,*
*So Fortune, like a master, rod in hand,*
*Raps our pates well to teach us how to live!*

***389.***

*Nor you nor I can read the etern decree,*
*To that enigma we can find no key;*

*They talk of you and me behtnd the veil,*
*But, if that veil be lifted, where are we?*

***390.***

*O Love, forever doth heaven's wheel design*
*To take away thy precious life, and mine;*
*Sit we upon this turf, 'twill not be long*
*'Ere turf shall grow upon my dust, and thine!*

***391.***

*When life has Bed, and we rest in the tomb,*
*They'll place a pair of bricks to mark our tomb;*
*And, a while after, mold our dust to bricks,*
*To furnish forth some other person's tomb!*

***392.***

*Yon palace, towering to the welkin blue,*
*Where kings did bow them down, and homage do,*
*I saw a ringdove on its arches perched,*
*And thus she made complaint, "Coo, Coo, Coo, Coo!"*

***393.***

*We come and go, but for the gain, where is it?*
*And spin life's woof, but for the warp, where is it?*
*And many a righteous man has burned to dust*
*In heaven's blue rondure, but their smoke, where is it?*

***394.***

*Life's well-spring lurks within that lip of thine!*
*Let not the cup's lip touch that lip of thine!*
*Beshrew me, if I fail to drink his blood,*
*For who is he, to touch that lip of thine?*

**395.**

*Such as I am, Thy power created me,*
*Thy care hath kept me for a century!*
*Through all these years I make experiment,*
*If my sins or Thy mercy greater be.*

**396.**

*"Take up thy cup and goblet, Love, " I said,*
*"Haunt purling river bank, and grassy glade;*
*Full many a moon-like form has heaven's wheel*
*Oft into cup, oft into goblet, made!"*

**397.**

*We buy new wine and old, our cups to fill,*
*And sell for two grains this world's good and ill;*
*Know you where you will go to after death?*
*Set wine before me, and go where you will!*

**398.**

*Was e'er man born who never went astray?*
*Did ever mortal pass a sinless day?*
*If I do ill, do not requite with ill!*
*Evil for evil how can'st Thou repay?*

**399.**

*Bring forth that ruby gem of Badakhshan,*
*That heart's delight, that balm of Turkestan;*
*They say 'tis wrong for Mussulmans to drink,*
*But ah! where can we find a Mussulman?*

**400.**

*My body's life and strength proceed from Thee!*
*My soul within and spirit are of Thee!*

*My being is of Thee, and Thou art mine,*
*And I am Thine, since I am lost in Thee!*

***401.***

*Man, like a ball, hither and thither goes,*
*As fate's resistless bat directs the blows;*
*But He, who gives thee up to this rude sport,*
*He knows what drives thee, yea, He knows, He knows!*

***402.***

*O Thou who givest sight to emmet's eyes,*
*And strength to puny limbs of feeble flies,*
*To Thee we will ascribe Almighty power,*
*And not base, unbecoming qualities.*

***403.***

*Let not base avarice enslave thy mind,*
*Nor vain ambition in its trammels bind;*
*Be sharp as fire, as running water swift,*
*Not, like earth's dust, the sport of every wind!*

***404.***

*'Tis best all other blessings to forego*
*For wine, that charming Turki maids bestow;*
*Kalendars' raptures pass all things that are,*
*From moon on high down into fish below!*

***405.***

*Friend! trouble not yourself about your lot,*
*Let futile care and sorrow be forgot;*
*Since this life's vesture crumbles into dust,*
*What matters stain of word or deed, or blot?*

***406.***

*O thou who hast done ill, and ill alone,*
*And thinkest to find mercy at the throne,*
*Hope not for mercy! for good left undone*
*Can not be done, nor evil done undone!*

***407.***

*Count not to live beyond your sixtieth year,*
*To walk in jovial courses persevere;*
*And ere your skull be turned into a cup,*
*Let wine-cups ever to your hand adhere!*

***408.***

*These heavens resemble an inverted cup,*
*Whereto the wise with awe keep gazing up;*
*So stoops the bottle o'er his love, the cup,*
*Feigning to kiss, and gives her blood to sup!*

***409.***

*I sweep the tavern threshold with my hair,*
*For both world's good and ill I take no care;*
*Should the two worlds roll to my house, like balls,*
*When drunk, for one small coin I'd sell the pair!*

***410.***

*The drop wept for his severance from the sea,*
*But the sea smiled, for "I am all," said he,*
*"The Truth is all, nothing exists beside,*
*That one point circling apes plurality. "*

***411.***

*Shall I still sigh for what I have not got,*
*Or try with cheerfulness to bear my lot?*

*Fill up my cup! I know not if the breath*
*I now am drawing is my last, or not!*

***412.***

*Yield not to grief, though fortune prove unkind,*
*Nor call sad thoughts of parted friends to mind;*
*Devote thy heart to sugary lips, and wine,*
*Cast not thy precious life unto the wind!*

***413.***

*Of mosque and prayer and fast preach not to me,*
*Rather go drink, were it on charity!*
*Yea, drink, Khayyam, your dust will soon be made*
*A jug, or pitcher, or a cup, may be!*

***414.***

*Bulbuls, doting on roses, oft complain*
*How froward breezes rend their veils in twain;*
*Sit we beneath this rose, which many a time*
*Has sunk to earth, and sprung from earth again.*

***415.***

*Suppose the world goes well with you, what then?*
*When life's last page is read and turned, what then?*
*Suppose you live a hundred years of bliss,*
*Yea, and a hundred years besides, what then?*

***416.***

*How is it that of all the leafy tribe,*
*Cypress and lily men as "free " describe?*
*This has a dozen tongues, yet holds her peace,*
*That has a hundred hands which take no bribe.*

***417.***

*Cupbearer, bring my wine-cup, let me grasp it!*
*Bring that delicious darling, let me grasp it!*
*That pleasing chain which tangles in its coils*
*Wise men and fools together, let me grasp it!*

***418.***

*Alas! my wasted life has gone to wrack!*
*What with forbidden meats, and lusts, alack!*
*And leaving undone what 'twas right to do,*
*And doing wrong, my face is very black!*

***419.***

*I could repent of all, but of wine, never!*
*I could dispense with all, but with wine, never!*
*If so be I became a Mussulman,*
*Could I abjure my Magian wine? no, never!*

***420.***

*We rest our hopes on Thy free grace alone,*
*Nor seek by merits for our sins to atone;*
*Mercy drops where it lists, and estimates*
*Ill done as undone, good undone as done.*

***421.***

*This is the form Thou gavest me of old,*
*Wherein Thou workest marvels manifold;*
*Can I aspire to be a better man,*
*Or other than I issued from Thy mold?*

***422.***

*O Lord! to Thee all creatures worship pay,*
*To Thee both small and great forever pray,*

*Thou takest woe away, and givest weal,*
*Give then, or, if it please Thee, take away!*

***423.***

*With going to and fro in this sad vale*
*Thou art grown double, and thy credit stale,*
*Thy nails are thickened like a horse's hoof,*
*Thy beard is ragged as an ass's tail.*

***424.***

*O unenlightened race of humankind,*
*Ye are a nothing, built on empty wind!*
*Yea, a mere nothing, hovering in the abyss,*
*A void before you, and a void behind!*

***425.***

*Each morn I say, "To-night I will repent*
*Of wine, and tavern-haunts no more frequent ";*
*But while 'tis spring, and roses are in bloom,*
*To loose me from my promise, O consent!*

***426.***

*Vain study of philosophy eschew!*
*Rather let tangled curls attract your view;*
*And shed the bottle's life-blood in your cup,*
*Or e'er death shed your blood, and feast on you.*

***427.***

*O heart! can'st thou the darksome riddle read,*
*Where wisest men have failed, wilt thou succeed?*
*Quaff wine, and make thy heaven here below,*
*Who knows if heaven above will be thy meed?*

***428.***

*They that have passed away, and gone before,*
*Sleep in delusion's dust for evermore;*
*Go, boy, and fetch some wine, this is the truth,*
*Their dogmas were but air, and wind their lore!*

***429.***

*O heart! when on the Loved One's sweets you feed,*
*You lose yourself, but find your Self indeed;*
*And, when you drink of His entrancing cup,*
*You hasten your escape from quick and dead!*

***430.***

*Though I am wont a wine-bibber to be,*
*Why should the people rail and chide at me?*
*Would that all evil actions made men drunk,*
*For then no sober people should I see!*

***431.***

*Child of four elements and sevenfold heaven,*
*Who fume and sweat because of these eleven,*
*Drink! I have told you seventy times and seven,*
*Once gone, nor hell will send you back, nor heaven.*

***432.***

*With many a snare Thou dost beset my way,*
*And threatenest, if I fall therein, to slay;*
*Thy rule resistless sways the world, yet Thou*
*Imputest sin, when I do but obey!*

***433.***

*To Thee, whose essence baffles human thought,*
*Our sins and righteous deeds alike seem naught;*

*May Thy grace sober me, though drunk with sins,*
*And pardon all the ill that I have wrought!*

**434.**

*If this life were indeed an empty play,*
*Each day would be an 'Iid of festal day,*
*And men might conquer all their hearts' desire,*
*Fearless of after penalties to pay!*

**435.**

*O wheel of heaven, you thwart my heart's desire,*
*And rend to shreds my scanty joy's attire,*
*The water that I drink you foul with earth,*
*And turn the very air I breathe to fire!*

**436.**

*O soul! could you but doff this flesh and bone,*
*You'd soar a sprite about the heavenly throne;*
*Had you no shame to leave your starry home,*
*And dwell an alien on this earthly zone?*

**437.**

*Ah, potter, stay thine hand! with ruthless art*
*Put not to such base use man's mortal part!*
*See, thou art mangling on thy cruel wheel*
*Faridun's fingers, and Kai Khosrau's heart!*

**438.**

*O rose! all beauties' charms thou dost excel,*
*As wine excels the pearl within its shell;*
*O fortune! thou dost ever show thyself*
*More strange, although I seem to know thee well!*

**439.**

*From this world's kitchen crave not to obtain*
*Those dainties, seeming real, but really vain,*
*Which greedy worldlings gorge to their own loss;*
*Renounce that loss, so loss shall prove thy gain!*

**440.**

*Plot not of nights, thy fellows' peace to blight,*
*So that they cry to God the live-long night;*
*Nor plume thee on thy wealth and might, which thieves*
*May steal by night, or death, or fortune's might.*

**441.**

*This soul of mine was once Thy cherished bride,*
*What caused Thee to divorce her from Thy side?*
*Thou didst not use to treat her thus of yore,*
*Why then now doom her in the world to abide?*

**442.**

*Ah! would there were a place of rest from pain,*
*Which we, poor pilgrims, might at last attain,*
*And after many thousand wintry years,*
*Renew our life, like flowers, and bloom again!*

**443.**

*While in love's book I sought an augury;*
*An ardent youth cried out in ecstasy,*
*"Who owns a sweetheart beauteous as the moon*
*Might wish his moments long as years to be!"*

**444.**

*Winter is past, and spring-tide has begun,*

*Soon will the pages of life's book be done!*
*Well saith the sage, "Life is a poison rank,*
*And antidote, save grape-juice, there is none. "*

***445.***

*Beloved, if thou a reverend Mullah be,*
*Quit saintly show, and feigned austerity,*
*And quaff the wine that Murtaza purveys,*
*And sport with Houris 'neath some shady tree!*

***446.***

*Last night I dashed my cup against a stone,*
*In a mad drunken freak, as I must own,*
*And lo! the cup cries out in agony,*
*"You too, like me, shall soon be overthrown."*

***447.***

*My heart is weary of hypocrisy,*
*Cupbearer, bring some wine, I beg of thee!*
*This hooded cowl and prayer-mat pawn for wine,*
*Then will I boast me in security.*

***448.***

*Audit yourself, your truce account to frame,*
*See! you go empty, as you empty came;*
*You say, "I will not drink and peril life,"*
*But, drink or no, you must die all the same!*

***449.***

*Open the door ! O entrance who procurest,*
*And guide the way, O Thou of guides the surest!*
*Directors born of men shall not direct me,*
*Their counsel comes to naught, but Thou endurest!*

***450.***

*In slandering and reviling you persist,*
*Calling me infidel and atheist:*
*My errors I will not deny, but yet*
*Does foul abuse become a moralist?*

***451.***

*To find a remedy, put up with pain,*
*Chafe not at woe, and healing thou wilt gain;*
*Though poor, be ever of a thankful mind,*
*'Tis the sure method riches to obtain.*

***452.***

*Give me a skin of wine, a crust of bread,*
*A pittance bare, a book of verse to read;*
*With thee, O love, to share my lowly roof,*
*I would not take the Sultan's realm instead!*

***453.***

*Reason not of the five, nor of the four,*
*Be their dark problems one, or many score;*
*We are but earth—Go, minstrel, bring the lute!*
*We are but air—Bring wine; I ask no more!*

***454.***

*Why argue on Yasin and on Barat?*
*Write me the draft for wine they call Barat!*
*The day my weariness is drowned in wine*
*Will seem to me as the great night Barat!*

***455.***

*Whilst thou dost wear this fleshy livery,*
*Step not beyond the bounds of destiny;*

*Bear up, though very Rustems be thy foes,*
*And crave no boon from friends like Hatim Tai!*

***456.***

*These ruby lips, and wine, and minstrel boys,*
*And lute, and harp, your dearly cherished toys,*
*Are mere redundancies, and you are naught,*
*'Till you renounce the world's delusive joys.*

***457.***

*Bow down, heaven's tyranny to undergo,*
*Quaff wine to face the world, and all its woe;*
*Your origin and end are both in earth,*
*But now you are above earth, not below!*

***458.***

*You know all secrets of this earthly sphere,*
*Why then remain a prey to empty fear?*
*You can not bend things to your will, but yet*
*Cheer up for the few moments you are here!*

***459.***

*Behold, where'er we turn our ravished eyes,*
*Sweet verdure springs, and crystal Kausars rise;*
*And plains, once bare as hell, now smile as heaven:*
*Enjoy this heaven with maids of Paradise!*

***460.***

*Never in this false world on friends rely,*
*(I give this counsel confidentially);*
*Put up with pain, and seek no antidote;*
*Endure your grief, and ask no sympathy!*

***461.***

*Of wisdom's dictates two are principal,*
*Surpassing all your lore traditional;*
*Better to fast than eat of every meat,*
*Better to live alone than mate with all!*

***462.***

*Why unripe grapes are sharp, prithee explain,*
*And then grow sweet, while wine is sharp again?*
*When one has carved a block into a lute,*
*Can he from that same block a pipe obtain?*

***463.***

*When dawn doth silver the dark firmament,*
*Why shrills the bird of dawning his lament?*
*It is to show in dawn's bright looking-glass*
*How of thy careless life a night is spent.*

***464.***

*Cupbearer, come! from thy full-throated ewer*
*Pour blood-red wine, the world's despite to cure!*
*Where can I find another friend like wine,*
*So genuine, so solacing, so pure?*

***465.***

*Though you should sit in sage Aristo's room,*
*Or rival Csesar on his throne of Rum,*
*Drain Jemshid's goblet, for your end's the tomb,*
*Yea, were you Bahram's self, your end's the tomb!*

***466.***

*It chanced into a potter's shop I strayed,*
*He turned his wheel and deftly plied his trade,*

*And out of monarchs' heads, and beggars' feet,*
*Fair heads and handles for his pitchers made!*

**467.**

*If you have sense, true senselessness attain,*
*And the Etern Cupbearer's goblet drain;*
*If not, true senselessness is not for you—*
*Not every fool true senselessness can gain!*

**468.**

*O Love! before you pass death's portal through,*
*And potters make their jugs of me and you,*
*Pour from this jug some wine, of headache void,*
*And fill your cup, and fill my goblet too!*

**469.**

*O Love! while yet you can, with tender art,*
*Lift sorrow's burden from your lover's heart;*
*Your wealth of graces will not always last,*
*But slip from your possession, and depart!*

**470.**

*Bestir thee, ere death's cup for thee shall flow,*
*And blows of ruthless fortune lay thee low;*
*Acquire some substance here, there is none there,*
*For those who thither empty-handed go!*

**471.**

*Who framed the lots of quick and dead but Thou?*
*Who turns the troublous wheel of heaven but Thou?*
*Though we are sinful slaves, is it for Thee*
*To blame us? Who created us but Thou?*

**472.**

*O wine, most limpid, pure, and crystalline,*
*Would I could drench this silly frame of mine*
*With thee, that passers-by might think 'twas thou,*
*And cry, "Whence comest thou, fair master wine?"*

**473.**

*A Shaikh beheld a harlot, and quoth he,*
*"You seem a slave to drink and lechery ";*
*And she made answer, "What I seem I am,*
*But, Master, are you all you seem to be? "*

**474.**

*If, like a ball, earth to my house were borne,*
*When drunk, I'd rate it at a balrleycorn;*
*Last night they offered me in pawn for wine,*
*But the rude vintner laughed that pledge to scorn.*

**475.**

*Now in thick clouds Thy face Thou dost immerse,*
*And now display it in this universe;*
*Thou the spectator, Thou the spectacle,*
*Sole to Thyself Thy glories dost rehearse.*

**476.**

*Better to make one soul rejoice with glee,*
*Than plant a desert with a colony;*
*Rather one freeman bind with chains of love,*
*Than set a thousand prisoned captives free!*

**477.**

*O thou who for thy pleasure dost impart*
*A pang of sorrow to thy fellow's heart,*

*Go! mourn thy perished wit, and peace of mind,*
*Thyself hast slain them, like the fool thou art!*

**478.**

*Wherever you can get two maunds of wine,*
*Set to, and drink it like a libertine;*
*Whoso acts thus will set his spirit free*
*From saintly airs like yours, and grief like mine.*

**479.**

*So long as I possess two maunds of wine,*
*Bread of the flower of wheat, and mutton chine,*
*And you, O Tulip cheek, to share my hut,*
*Not every Sultan's lot can vie with mine.*

**480.**

*They call you wicked, if to fame you're known,*
*And an intriguer, if you live alone;*
*Trust me, though you were Khizr or Elias,*
*'Tis best to know none, and of none be known.*

**481.**

*Yes! here am I with wine and feres again!*
*I did repent, but, ah! 'twas all in vain;*
*Preach not to me of Noah and his flood,*
*But pour a flood of wine to drown my pain!*

**482.**

*For union with my love I sigh in vain,*
*The pangs of absence I can scarce sustain,*
*My grief I dare not tell to any friend;*
*O trouble strange, sweet passion, bitter pain!*

***483.***

*'Tis dawn! I hear the loud Muezzin's call,*
*And here am I before the vintner's hall;*
*This is no time of piety. Be still!*
*And drop your talk and airs devotional!*

***484.***

*Angel of joyful foot! the dawn is nigh;*
*Pour wine, and lift your tuneful voice on high,*
*Sing how Jemshids and Khosraus bit the dust,*
*Whelmed by the rolling months, from Tir to Dai!*

***485.***

*Frown not at revelers, I beg of thee,*
*For all thou keepest righteous company;*
*But drink, for, drink or no, 'tis all the same,*
*If doomed to hell, no heaven thou'lt ever see.*

***486.***

*I wish that Allah would rebuild these skies,*
*And earth, and that at once, before my eyes,*
*And either 'rase my name from off his roll,*
*Or else relieve my dire necessities!*

***487.***

*Lord! make thy bounty's cup for me to flow,*
*And bread unbegged for day by day bestow;*
*Yea, with thy wine make me beside myself.*
*No more to feel the headache of my woe!*

***488.***

*Omar! of burning heart, perchance to burn*
*In hell, and feed its bale-fires in thy turn,*

*Presume not to teach Allah clemency,*
*For who art thou to teach, or He to learn?*

***489.***

*Cheer up! your lot was settled yesterday!*
*Heedless of all that you might do or say,*
*Without so much as "By your leave" they fixed*
*Your lot for all the morrows yesterday!*

***490.***

*I never would have come, had I been asked,*
*I would as lief not go, if I were asked,*
*And, to be short, I would annihilate*
*All coming, being, going, were I asked!*

***491.***

*Man is a cup, his soul the wine therein,*
*Flesh is a pipe, spirit the voice within;*
*O Khayyam, have you fathomed what man is?*
*A magic lantern with a light therein!*

***492.***

*O skyey wheel, all base men you supply*
*With baths, mills, and canals that run not dry,*
*While good men have to pawn their goods for bread:*
*Pray, who would give a fig for such a sky?*

***493.***

*A potter at his work I chanced to see,*
*Pounding some earth and shreds of pottery;*
*I looked with eyes of insight, and methought*
*'Twas Adam's dust with which he made so free!*

***494.***

*The Saki knows my* genus *properly,*
*To all woe's species he holds a key;*
*Whene'er my mood is sad he brings me wine,*
*And that makes all the difference to me!*

***495.***

*Dame Fortune! all your acts and deeds confess*
*That you are foul oppression's votaress;*
*You cherish bad men, and annoy the good;*
*Is this from dotage, or sheer foolishness?*

***496.***

*You, who in carnal lusts your time employ,*
*Wearing your precious spirit with annoy,*
*Know that these things you set your heart upon*
*Sooner or later must the soul destroy!*

***497.***

*Hear from the spirit-world this mystery:*
*Creation is summed up, O man, in thee;*
*Angel and demon, man and beast art thou,*
*Yea, thou art all thou dost appear to be!*

***498.***

*If popularity you would ensue,*
*Speak well of Muslim, Christian, and Jew;*
*So shall you be esteemed of great and small,*
*And none will venture to speak ill of you.*

***499.***

*O wheel of heaven, what have I done to you,*
*That you should thus annoy me? Tell me true;*

*To get a drink I have to cringe and stoop,*
*And for my bread you make me beg and sue.*

***500.***

*No longer hug your grief and vain despair,*
*But in this unjust world be just and fair;*
*And since the issue of the world is naught,*
*Think you are naught, and so shake off dull care!*

# Bibliography


Arnold, Sir Thomas W.: *Painting in Islam: A Study of the Place of Pictorial Art in Muslim Culture*, New York, 1965.

Atil, Esin: *Exhibition of 2500 Years of Persian Art*, Washington D.C., 1971.

Bayat, Mojdeh: *Tales from the Land of the Sufis,* Boston, Mass., Shambhala Publications, 1994.

Bly, Robert: *When Grapes Turn to Wine,* Cambridge, Mass., Yellow Moon Press, 1986

Browne, Edward Granville: *A Persian Anthology: Being Translations From the Persian,* London, E. Benn, 1927.

Chandra, Moti: *The Technique of Mughal Painting*, Lucknow, 1949.

Cave, George.*Sufi Poetry*. Rawalpindin, Pakistan, R.C.D. Cultural Association, 1986.

Chittick, William: *The Sufi Path of Love: the Spiritual Teaching of Rumi.* N.Y., State University of New York Press, 1983.

Cowan, James: *Where Two Oceans Meet: A Selection of Odes from the Divan of Shems of Tabriz,* Rockport, Mass., Element, 1992.

Curzon, George N.: *Persia and the Persian Question*, London, 1892.

DeLamotte, Roy C.: *Jalaluddin Rumi, Songbird of Sufism,* Lanham, Md., University Press of America, 1980.

Dole, Nathan Haskell: *Flowers from Persian Poets,* New York, Thomas Y. Crowell, 1901.

Ergin, Nevit Oguz: *Crazy as We Are: Selected Rubais from Divan-i Kebir,* Prescott, Ariz., Hohn Press, 1992.

Ernst, Carl: *Teaching Sufism,* Boston, Shambhala Press, 1999.

Feild, Reshad: *The Last Barrier: A Sufi Journey*, Rockport, Element, 1993

Guest, Grace Dunham: *Shiraz Painting in the Sixteenth Century*, Washington D.C., 1948.

Guvenc, R. Oruc: *Lovers of God, Mevlana*, Vaduz, Liechtenstein, Aconcagua, 1986.

Hakim, Khalifa Abdul: *The Metaphysics of Rumi, a Critical and Historical Sketch,* Lahore, Pakistan, Institute of Islamic Culture, 1959.

Holter, Kurt: *Persische Miniaturen*, Vienna, 1921.

Losty, J. P.: *The Art of the Book in India*, London, 1982.

Lowry, Glenn, and Nemazee, Susan: *A Jeweler's Eye: Islamic Arts of the Book from the Vever Collection*, Washington D.C., 1988.

Robinson, B. W.: *A Descriptive Catalogue of the Persian Paintings in the Bodleian Library*, Oxford, 1958.

Robinson, B. W.: *Islamic Painting and the Arts of the Book*, London: 1976.

Rohani, Nasrin: *A Bibliography of Persian Miniature Painting*, Boston, 1982.

Schimmel, Annemarie: *Calligraphy and Islamic Culture*, New York, 1984.

Schmitz Barbara: *Islamic Manuscripts in the New York Public Library*, New York, 1992.

Schmitz Barbara: *Islamic and Indian Manuscripts and Paintings in the Pierpont Morgan Library*, New York, 1997.

Titıey, Norah M.: *Persian Miniature Painting and its Influence on the Art of Turkey and India*, Austin, 1984.

Welch, Stuart Cary: *Artists for the Shah: Late Sixteenth-Century Painting at the Imperial Court of Iran*, New Haven, 1976.

Welch, S. C., and Dickinson, Martin B.: *The Houghton Shahnameh*, Cambridge, 1981.

Welch, S. C., and Welch, Anthony: *Arts of the Islamic Book: The Collection of Prince Sadruddin Aga Khan*, Ithaca, 1982.

Yarshater, Ehsan: *Encyclopaedia Iranica*, London, 1982.

# INDEX

## D



## E



## F



## G



## H

## I



## J



## K



## L



## M



## N



## O

## P



## R



## S